A TREASURY OF

Scottie

Dog

Collectibles

IDENTIFICATION & VALUES
VOLUME II

CANDACE STEN DAVIS

PATRICIA J. BAUGH

COLLECTOR BOOKS
A Division of Schroeder Publishing Co., Inc.

In this volume we have listed values/price ranges for most items. We have determined these prices from what we have paid or observed in today's marketplace. The authors and the publisher assume no responsibility for any losses which may occur as a result of using values set forth in this volume. Prices we have stated are for an item in excellent or mint condition. Prices should be significantly reduced if an item is damaged or badly worn.

Collectors and sellers should use these values as a guide, not as an absolute. Assigning "book value" to an item is a mistake. Condition, availability, and the desire of the purchaser affect the price of an item; book prices are but suggestions.

Beware of reproductions and unscrupulous dealers who try to offer you a new item that has been "aged." Education is your best defense against these people. When you collect something like Scotties, you must be knowledgeable in every type of collectible as Scotties appear in most every medium. Antique related publications will help you make wise decisions when determining whether an item offered to you is worth the asking price.

Remember, the value of an item is the price most recently agreed upon between the buyer and the seller.

Searching For A Publisher?

We are always looking for knowledgeable people considered to be experts within their fields. If you feel that there is a real need for a book on your collectible subject and have a large comprehensive collection, contact Collector Books.

Front cover: Top left: Doll, 8", Jean's Dolls, Wendy Walks Her Dog, Madame Alexander, circa 1980s, $100.00 – 150.00 (c); **Top right:** Hooked Rug, wool, Angus Stitches, made by Candee Davis, circa 1990s (c); **Center:** 1½" x 4" x 3", blue carnival glass, marked "R.M. St. Clair, Elwood, Ind.," circa 1979, $150.00 – 200.00 (c); **Bottom left:** Bookends, 4¾" x 5", cast iron, Hubley No. 430, circa 1930 – 1940s, $275.00 – 350.00 (c); **Bottom right:** Three Dimensional Collector Plate, "A Family At Last," *Lady and the Tramp*, Disney, circa 1995, limited edition of 7,500, $75.00 – 100.00 (c).

Cover design by Beth Summers
Book layout by Mary Ann Hudson

COLLECTOR BOOKS
P.O. Box 3009
Paducah, Kentucky 42002-3009

Contents

Dedications

To my husband, who makes my life complete — to my family, who fills my days with memories — and to all Scottie collectors who have made Volume II possible.
Candace (Candee) Sten Davis

To my father, Don Baugh, my sister and brother-in-law, Tammy Baugh and Mark Swessinger, and my "very best good friend," Susan Mayfield, each of whom I love dearly, I dedicate this book.
Patricia (Patty) Baugh

About the Authors

A Scottie life ... her parents met because of two Scotties; she was born in Hyde Park, New York, home of Fala, the most famous Scottie, who owned Franklin D. Roosevelt; her husband Ken, a technical writer, gave her an antique Scottie pin on their honeymoon; their first home was just down the street from Wilderstein, the home of FDR's cousin, Margaret Suckley, where she trained Fala for FDR; and living and representations of Scotties have populated Candee and Ken's home for over 20 years. Candee owns and operates several small businesses including Scottie Treasures, Nana's Cottage, Fancywork, and Angus Stitches. They have two children, Colleen and Joshua, and two grandchildren, Courtney Moriah and Nicholas Tyler. Their children's spouses, Jeremy and Tammee, complete their family. Candee and Ken share their 200+ year old country Victorian home with Angus Macbeth, Emily MacKenzie, Clementine (a daschund/terrier), and three cats, Jasper, Hillary, and Tessa Noelle.

Candee would like to introduce her new little lady, Emily MacKenzie... who obviously loves the snowy New York weather. She did not help with this volume as she arrived after work was completed... but we thought you would like to meet the newest Scottie addition in the Davis home.

Patty Baugh was raised in Joy, Illinois, and spent her childhood in the company of dachshunds. A musician and teacher by trade, her passion is collecting. Toby came to live with her in 1992 after she discovered that her dog allergy did not include cairn terriers. She rescued Rocky, another cairn, in 1997. A Grape Nuts creamer reminded her of Toby and that purchase was the beginning of her Scottie obsession. A conversation with her Aunt Julia revealed that Patty's grandmother

had purchased three boxes of Grape Nuts cereal in the late 30s so that each of her daughters could have one of the free creamers that came in the box. Her aunt believed that the collection started with Patty's late mother's creamer, but that one is long gone. Patty had more than made up for it with a collection of over 50 of the creamers by the time she heard this story! Now the Scotties multiply regularly and she is thrilled to be able to share them with you!

Acknowledgments

We would like to thank the following people for their time, effort, and support with our second volume of *A Treasury of Scottie Dog Collectibles.*

Ken Davis, Candee's husband, who photographed her collection and the collection of Marion and Fred Krupp.

Ken Davis

Candee thanks her family for posing in Scottie clothing, especially the lights of her life, Courtney Moriah Evans Davis Lauer and Nicholas Tyler Lauer.

We thank Marion and Fred Krupp, who allowed us to photograph a part of their collection. They have been collecting Scotties for 26 years after Peggy, their first Scottie, joined their family a year after they married. Their landlord visited New Hope, Pennsylvania, and brought them a small Scottie figurine. Ironically, they soon moved to the New Hope area and have been there for over 25 years. Marion has been an artist since the age of 13 and Fred recently retired from AT&T. Marion's work appears in many permanent collections including the Dog Museum of America and the Philadelphia Zoological Society's Primate Center, and in many private collections throughout the world. Her work has earned her many awards through the years, and has captured the hearts of animal lovers world-wide. Their present furry family is shown with them: Clara, a wirehaired dachshund, and Cassy, Hobbes, and Calvin. Photograph courtesy of Nancy Xander.

Marion and Fred Krupp with the dogs from left to right: Clara, Cassy, Hobbes & Calvin.

Many thanks to Patty's 350+ students who bring Scottie goodies to her and fill her days with hugs and smiles.

Patty thanks Paul Hayes of Paul's Studio and Photo Express in Moline for all his help in training this truly novice photographer.

Patty thanks Toby for being such a sweet little guy and her constant companion for the last seven years. Rocky gets kudos for sniffing every item she photographed, helping at the computer as she and Candee did this book, talking constantly, and generally keeping life very interesting for her and Toby.

Toby & Rocky

Candee would also like to thank Angus Macbeth for inspecting every item before it was photographed, moving the table to make photographing a real challenge, and brightening every day; he is a member of our family.

Angus Macbeth

We thank our editor, Lisa Stroup, for accepting and supporting our second volume. Her kindness and encouragement are greatly appreciated. Gracious thanks to the Collector Books staff as well. Working with you has been a pleasure.

Introduction

Welcome to *A Treasury of Scottie Dog Collectibles, Volume II.* If you have Volume I, you will find that there are no exact duplications in Volume II, only examples of variations in color or medium. If you don't have Volume I, at the time of this printing it is still available from the publisher or your local bookstore, or it can be ordered from Candee. With both books in your library you will not have a complete listing of all the Scottie Dog collectibles available, but you will have access to photographs and information covering over 1,500 different Scottie dog collectibles!

As with our first book, we want to make it clear that we are not experts in the field of Scottie Dog Collectibles. We are simply Scottie collectors who are making available to you a sampling of what is out in the marketplace now and what has been available in the past. If you have items in your collection that we haven't shown in either volume, please send us photographs. We are already working on Volume III!

This book is set up in the same chapter format as the last, to aid you in locating items. We duplicate information only in the "Book Lists" and "Scottie Sightings in the Movies," so you can avoid having to consult both volumes for that information.

We have included new and old items in our books. They are collectible guides, not just antique guides. Just because an item is new and available doesn't guarantee that it will be available in the near future. We have seen items rise quickly in value in just a few months. For example, the Timex miniature clock that was offered at the end of 1997 is selling for a minimum of twice the offering price now. Choose wisely if you are investing in Scottie items for future profit, or buy them all if you want to fill your home with these adorable little dogs! The wealth of Scottie Collectibles is endless; at least we hope it is! For many, the fun in collecting is "the search." We wish you good luck in your quest for Scottie collectibles, new or old. Whether you are a beginning collector or a seasoned veteran, we hope you enjoy our efforts and we look forward to hearing from you.

Candace L. Sten Davis
P.O. Box 130
Slaterville Springs, NY 14881
e-mail: fancywork@clarityconnect.com

Patricia J. Baugh
561 Oaklawn Avenue
E. Moline, IL 61244
e-mail: flamingo@qconline.com

Care and Feeding of Scottie Collectibles

The purchase of a book such as this one will help the collector to become more informed as to what is available and approximately what one should pay for an item.

However, once the item has arrived home and the excitement of the find has subsided, the dirt and grime begin to show. We offer here some suggestions on the care and feeding of your Scottie collection.

When cleaning an item that is ceramic, porcelain, glass or china, it is best to use mild soap and water. Do not use modern cleaning products, and do not put any vintage dishes in the dishwasher. Test the finish in an area that is not readily noticeable before beginning to clean, even with water, especially for any item that has decals or hand painting. Patty learned at a very early date in her collecting that immersing an item with decals is not a good idea. Thus the loss of a Scottie tail on her cube lamp! When removing price labels from these mediums, the use of a product called Goo Gone has been recommended and works well, but Patty finds that the best thing to remove a label is creamy peanut butter. Rub a little on the label, wait until the oil saturates, and it should come off easily. Repeat if necessary. Once you have the label and grime removed, keep the collectible clean by wiping with a damp cloth and use a soft cloth to dry thoroughly.

Celluloid, Bakelite, and other early plastics need special care. Make certain that these items are in a dry, well ventilated space. Use a mild soap to remove any dirt, but as suggested before, always test the back of the item first. We do not recommend submerging items with glued decorations in water. If the pin finding is broken or missing, Aileen's Tacky Glue and a new pin finding, both available at craft stores, have proven successful for Patty.

Wood items should be cared for like fine furniture. Test an inconspicuous spot and then use a mild solution of Murphy's Oil Soap and water, again being careful with decals, and dry completely with a soft cloth. Composition wood items seem to be very hearty and this method will usually do the trick. Do not immerse wood items in the water.

Paper should be stored in an acid free environment. Acid free supplies are readily available through stationery and craft stores. If you find an item that has been taped, think twice before purchasing it. Tape will break down the paper and destroy your item. If there are labels on the paper, be cautious about purchasing it. The glue on a label will not come off of the paper and will eventually destroy it. Patty found a coloring book that had tape on the back and it was priced at $3.00. She bought it, but when she found a Peggy Brown book that was heavily taped and overpriced even for a mint item, she did not buy it. She wanted it, but the tape would have ultimately destroyed the book.

Linens must also be stored in an acid free, dry, well-ventilated environment. It is best to hand wash the items. Use a mild soap and water, test first on a corner and when finished washing, make sure that the soap is rinsed out completely. If there are stains, try a solution of color safe bleach, baking soda, and water. Apply to the stain and let it sit in cold water overnight, then wash with warm water and mild soap. Roll in a towel and gently press out excess water, then lay flat on a dry towel and shape the item. When dry, iron on the wrong side with a towel underneath, using a pressing cloth on top to protect the linen. Do

not use starch as this will damage the fibers. Linens that are not displayed should be stored rolled, not folded, between sheets of acid free tissue paper.

When purchasing metal items, we suggest that you clean off dirt and grime with the usual mild soap and water and dry it thoroughly. Do not try to polish or restore the surface of the metal. If you destroy the patina, the value of the item will plummet. Enjoy that aged patina of your older metal Scottie items, but be aware that there are unscrupulous dealers who will try to "age" a new item.

Proper care of your Scottie dog collectibles will ensure your enjoyment of them for many years. This overview is by no means a complete guide on the care and feeding of Scottie dog collectibles, but we hope it will help you keep those adorable pooches clean and happy!

Displaying Scottie Collectibles

We are sure you have found many creative ways to display and use your Scotties around your home, but just in case you haven't, we have a few suggestions.

Candee and Ken have a large, old house and have other collections besides their Scotties. Their Scottie bookends support their book collection throughout the house. Miniature Scotties, like the Monopoly game pieces, roam around their Christmas village at holiday time. Key rings and small statues receive ribbons and adorn wreaths and garlands decorating doors at holiday time and all year round. Quilts hang on the walls for decoration and to protect from winter drafts. Plush Scotties fill the crib their grandchildren have outgrown, but the "Anguses" come out to keep them company in "big beds" when they visit. Candee has tucked a Scottie doorstop in the corner of each stair tread and she uses a group of vintage powder boxes for jewelry boxes in the bedrooms, and to hold powder, soap, and cotton balls in the bathroom. To keep her collection of Scottie pins visible, Candee has framed a velvet covered board where she displays her Scottie jewelry. This makes choosing the right fellow much easier than jewelry box storage, and it makes a vivid wall decoration. Candee enjoys hooking rugs and has some antique ones as well. Little by little she is creating a "wall to wall" carpet of Scotties in her office.

Patty, on the other hand, lives in a very small house, but also has many other collections. In the

kitchen her blue china and cobalt glass are displayed with a variety of blue Scotties interspersed throughout. Grouping her "army" of 50+ Grape Nuts creamers on one shelf with Morton sugar and creamers makes for a visual surprise. She uses these creamers throughout the entire house to catch jewelry, pens, or other stray items. They are also used for nuts, mints, silverware, and, surprise, cream for coffee when she entertains. Cigarette boxes are used for jewelry and a humidor holds cotton swabs. The living room has a cabinet and a child's hutch made by her grandfather, now devoted to Scotties. Two antique high chairs and the teeter totter shown in the Toys section are covered with stuffed fellows. Grouped on her piano is a collection of Scottie lamps, with musical themed Scotties dancing in their spotlights.

Try stacking tartan hat boxes of varying sizes and place your fellows around the edges and add a plush Scottie peeking out of the top box. Use your Scottie linens as curtains, draped on pressure rods fitted into your window frames. Create a unique display by framing your favorite Scottie greeting cards. Change the cards on a seasonal or holiday basis.

We see our collections every day and rearrange parts on a regular basis, finding new ways to display our favorites of the moment. We would love to see how you have displayed your collection. Please send photographs!

Picture Codes and Arrangement

At the end of each description is a letter code in parentheses. These codes are used to denote owner and photographer of the item, respectively,
   (c) Candace Sten Davis; Ken Davis
   (p) Patricia J. Baugh; Patricia J. Baugh
   (k) Marion and Fred Krupp; Ken Davis

We have, for the most part, arranged each section according to material used to create the item. Primarily, items are shown in the following order: ceramic/plaster/porcelain, composition, glass, metal, wood, and combinations.

Fala

Undeniably the most famous Scottie of our time, Fala remains a favorite among Scottie lovers. Our 32nd President, Franklin Delano Roosevelt, was owned by this Scottish terrier, known formally as Murray, the Outlaw of Fala Hill. Fala often traveled with FDR and was his constant companion in the White House. He remained with Eleanor Roosevelt after the President's death in April 1945. Fala passed away on April 5, 1952, two days before his twelfth birthday, and was laid to rest at his master's side in the Rose Garden at Hyde Park. It was FDR's wish that his loving companion always be close.

Postcard, Fala at the grave site of his master, Franklin D. Roosevelt, circa 1947, $15.00 – 20.00 (c).

Limited Edition Signed Print, "Hold On Fala," Artist: Marion Needham Krupp, circa 1997, $75.00 – 100.00 (k).

Print, "Watch Your Step," Artist: Marion Needham Krupp, circa 1998, $40.00 – 50.00 (c).

Cards, Artist: E. N. Fairchild, illustrations from *The True Story of Fala*, by M. L. Suckley and A. Dalgliesh, circa 1990s, $1.00 – 3.00 (c).

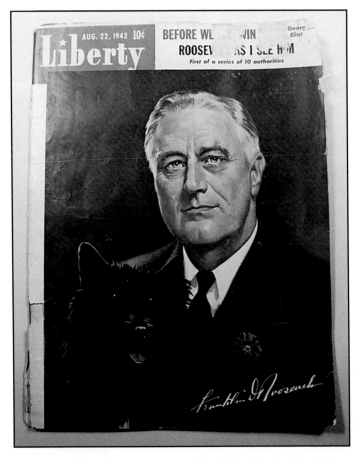

Liberty Magazine, circa August 22, 1942, $20.00 – 35.00 (k).

Christmas Ornament, pewter, Roosevelt – Vanderbilt Historical Association series, circa 1997, $15.00 (c).

Fala Fob, sterling silver, circa 1940s, $40.00 – 50.00 (k). Note: FDR ordered 212 of these from Hammacher Schlemmer for Christmas gifts.

Ashtray, 3" x 4½", ceramic, souvenir of FDR's home in Hyde Park, New York, circa 1960s, $50.00 – 60.00 (k).

Tumbler, 5", glass, souvenir of Roosevelt's home in Hyde Park, New York, circa 1940s, $15.00 – 20.00 (p).

Playing Cards, Fala and Roosevelt/Vanderbilt mansions, paper, circa 1990s, $10.00 – 20.00 (c).

Dolls, FDR, Eleanor, and Fala, Artist: Gladys Boalt, circa 1990s, $80.00 – 100.00 (k).

Magazine Article, *Movie Radio Guide Monthly*, circa June 1943, $15.00 – 20.00 (p).

Postage Stamp, Federated States of Micronesia, circa 1998, $10.00 – 20.00 (c).

Postcard, "Petey & Fala," Petey owns Jimmy Stallings, taken at the FDR Memorial in Washington, D.C., photo first appeared in *Good Dog* magazine, Photographer: Ross Becker, Printed in the USA by Concept II Graphics and Printing, Inc., circa 1998, $1.00 (c).

Banks

These thrifty Scots will hold your coins until the next Scottie collectible comes your way!

4" x 2¾" x 5", composition, circa 1930s, $25.00 – 60.00 (c).

7½", plastic, Reliable, circa 1950 – 1960s, $60.00 – 80.00 (k).

2½" x 3¾" x 4½", metal, circa 1930s, $25.00 – 60.00 (c).

2½" x 3½" x 5½", metal, circa 1930s, $25.00 – 60.00 (c).

2¾" x 4" x 5", flocked metal, circa 1930s, $25.00 – 60.00 (c).

3" x 4" x 5", metal, circa 1930s,
$25.00 – 60.00 (c).

6½" x 4" x 6¼", metal, marked "Vanio," circa 1935,
$40.00 – 65.00 (c).

8 Ball, 4" x 3½" x 3½", metal, circa 1950s, $80.00 –
125.00 (k).

2½" x 4½" x 5", metal, $60.00 – 80.00 (k).

Bookends

Scottie bookends come in just about any form or medium you can imagine. They work diligently keeping your library organized, and the best part of bookend collecting is that you get *two* Scotties for the price of one! All prices are per pair.

4½" x 5½", composition, circa 1940s, $30.00 – 60.00 (c).

5" x 4" x 4", flocked chalk, marked "Made in Japan," circa 1950s, $15.00 – 20.00 (p).

4" x 3" x 6", chalk, circa 1950s, $25.00 – 40.00 (c).

2½" x 6½" x 5", glass, Corning, Squatty Scottie, circa 1940s, $75.00 – 125.00 (c). These have been reissued in recent years. The newer version has a greenish cast and sells for approximately half the selling price of the vintage version.

2½" x 3¼" x 4¼", metal, marked "Made in Japan," circa 1940s, $50.00 – 75.00 (c).

4" x 3½", cast iron/silver wash, Hubley No. 434, circa 1930 – 1940s, $250.00 – 300.00 (c).

6" x 2¼" x 5½", bronze clad gray metal, marked "Pompeian Bronze," circa 1920s, $200.00 – 250.00 (c).

3¾" x 2¼" x 5⅛", metal, marked "B&H," Bradley & Hubbard, circa 1920 – 1930s, $60.00 – 100.00 (c).

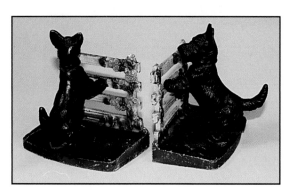

4¾" x 5", cast iron, Hubley No. 430, circa 1930 – 1940s, $275.00 – 350.00 (c).

3" x 4½" x 6½", metal, circa 1940 – 1950s, $50.00 – 75.00 (c).

5" x 4" x 5¾", metal/enameled, circa 1940s, $20.00 – 40.00 (c). Note: picture adapted from etching done in 1923, "Pals," by Marguerite Kirmse.

4½" x 4" x 6", metal, marked "Frankart," circa 1940s, $100.00 – 125.00 (c).

5½" x 3½" x 4½", cast iron, circa 1940s, $60.00 – 80.00 (k).

5" x 2½" x 4½", metal, Bradley & Hubbard, circa 1920s, $180.00 – 200.00 (k).

5" x 2½" x 4½", metal, marked "B&H," Bradley & Hubbard, circa 1920s, $110.00 – 130.00 (k).

3¼" x 3½" x 6", metal, Dodge, circa 1940s, $100.00 – 125.00 (k).

7⁄8" x 2" x 5", metal/marble base, circa 1960s, $80.00 – 110.00 (k).

5½" x 3" x 4¾", cast iron, Hubley No. 263, circa 1940s, $125.00 – 150.00 (k).

5" x 5" x 3", pot metal, circa 1940s, $35.00 – 45.00 (p).

5" x 3" x 3", bronze/marble, circa 1930s, $25.00 – 35.00 (p).

4" x 4½" x 5", metal, circa 1940 – 1950s, $25.00 – 50.00 (c).

6" x 4" x 3", metal, Nuart, circa 1930s, $35.00 – 40.00 (p).

5" x 3" x 4", metal, circa 1940 – 1950s, $25.00 – 50.00 (c).

5" x 5" x 7½", cast iron, Department 56, made in China, circa 1990s, $30.00 – 50.00 (c).

3" x 6" x 6", wood, circa 1930s, $50.00 – 75.00 (c).

A great variety of Scottie items exist that can organize your desk top. Let them help with your paperwork and it will give you more time to Scottie shop!

Clock, 4" x 1½" x 4¼", metal, Lux Clock Mfg., Waterbury, Connecticut, USA, circa 1930s, $120.00 – 150.00 (k).

Clock, 5" x 3" x 6", wood, Oswald Roving Eye, $375.00 – 450.00 (k).

Clock, 2½" x 1½" x 6", composition/metal, Lux Clock Mfg., Waterbury, Connecticut, USA, circa 1930s, $200.00 – 250.00 (k).

Clock, 3" x 1¼" x 2½", Timex, modeled after Scottie issued by Christofile Silversmiths of France, circa 1997, $50.00 – 75.00 (c).

Covered Dish, 3½" x 2⅞" x 2", silver on frosted glass, circa 1940s, $60.00 – 80.00 (k).

Letter Holder, 6" x 4" x 6", tin, Decal Artist: Lilian Chariot, circa 1940s, $30.00 – 50.00 (c).

Letter Holder, 4" x 2" x 4", metal, circa 1940s, $25.00 – 40.00 (c).

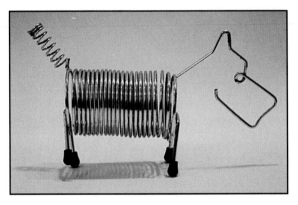

Letter holder, 9" x 5" x 2½", metal, Scotty-Terry "Watchful Secretary," Capitol Metal Products, circa 1950s, $12.00 – 15.00 (p).

Pen Holder/Calendar, 3½" x 3½" x 7", metal/Lucite, circa 1930s, $35.00 – 40.00 (p).

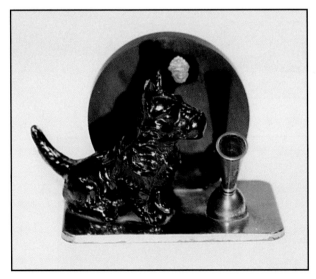

Pen Holder, 2½" x 1¾" x 2", brass/cast iron/Bakelite, marked "Hershey, Derby, Connecticut," $40.00 – 60.00 (c).

Pen Holder, 2½" x 2½", chrome/cast iron, circa 1940s, $20.00 – 30.00 (c).

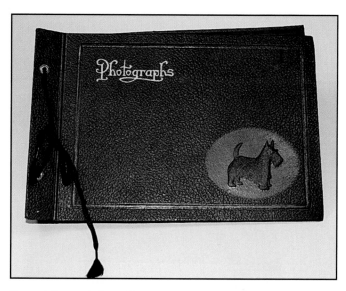

Pen Holder, 2½" x 2½" x 2", cast iron, marked "JB," Jennings Bros., circa 1930s, $45.00 – 50.00 (p).

Photo Album, 7¼" x 11", paper, circa 1940s, $25.00 – 50.00 (c).

Photo Album, 3" x 5", leather/paper, circa 1930s, $10.00 – 15.00 (p).

Picture Frame, 5" x 4", metal, circa 1990s, $5.00 – 10.00 (c).

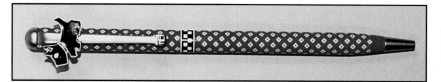

Pen, Artist: Mary Engelbreit, circa 1990s, $15.00 – 25.00 (c).

Box, 9" x 5" x 3", metal, marked "J.B.," Jennings Bros., circa 1930s, $75.00 – 100.00 (c).

Trinket Box, 7¼" x 4" x 4¾", bronze/marble, Phidias, $350.00 – 375.00 (k).

Covered 8 Ball Dish, 4" x 3½" x 3½", metal, circa 1950s, $80.00 – 125.00 (k).

Paperweight, 4" x 2" x 2", cast iron, Hubley No. 442, circa 1940s, $200.00 – 275.00 (k).

Paperweight, 3" x ¾" x 3", brass, marked "made in England," circa 1940s, $15.00 – 18.00 (p).

Rubber Stamp, Inkadinkado, Inc., 1987, $10.00 – 20.00 (c).

Notepad Holder for sticky notes, 4" x 3½" x 3", Lucite, circa 1990s, $12.00 – 15.00 (p).

Letter Holder/Thermometer, 5" x 1¾" x 3¾", wood, marked "Souvenir of Monroe, Mich.," circa 1950s, $20.00 – 30.00 (c).

Lap Board, 12" x 16", wood/fabric, circa 1980s, $20.00 – 30.00 (c).

Book Rack, 10" x 6" x 6", wood, circa 1970s, $20.00 – 40.00 (c).

Pencil Box, 11" x 4" x 2", cardboard/vinyl, circa 1940s, $20.00 – 25.00 (p).

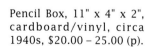

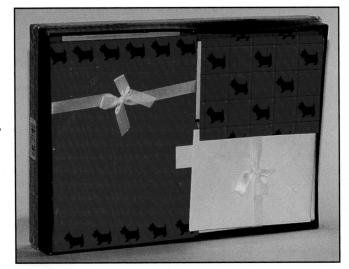

Stationery, 8½" x 11" x 1½", paper, circa 1990s, $10.00 – 15.00 (p).

Postage Stamp, circa 1994, $5.00 – 10.00 (c).

Postage Stamp, St. Vincent & The Grenadines, circa 1990s, $25.00 – 30.00 (c).

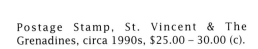

Postage Stamp, St. Vincent & The Grenadines, circa 1990s, $25.00 – 30.00 (c).

Scotties will hold open the door for us while protecting the domicile. Some of these fellows have held many doors open over the years, but they still do their job with the tenacity of the Scottish terrier.

Doorstop, 6" x 3" x 4", composition, circa 1940s, $20.00 – 30.00 (c).

Doorstop, 9" x 4" x 5½", cast iron, Hubley No. 447, circa 1940s, $200.00 – 250.00 (k).

Doorstop, 9" x 3" x 8", cast iron, circa 1940s, $150.00 – 200.00 (c).

Back view of photo on left (c).

Doorstops, 8" x 3½" x 8", cast iron, $80.00 – 120.00 (k).

Doorstop, 8" x 2½" x 5½", brass, circa 1950s, $40.00 – 75.00 (c).

Doorstop, 6½" x 6½" x 2½", metal, marked "made in China," circa 1990s, $10.00 – 20.00 (p).

Doorstop, 7" x 2½" x 7", cast iron, circa 1990s, $15.00 – 30.00 (c).

Boot Scraper, 7" x 4" x 7", cast iron, circa 1940s, $100.00 – 150.00 (c).

Boot Scraper, 10½" x 4", bronze, $100.00 – 150.00 (k).

Boot Scraper, 10" x 5", cast iron, circa 1970, $40.00 – 60.00 (k).

Boot Scraper, 10" x 3", cast iron, $75.00 – 100.00 (k).

What better way to shed a little light on the subject than to use a Scottie lamp!

2" x 3" x 5", chalkware; shade 4"/paper, circa 1940s, $75.00 – 100.00 (c).

6" x 5½" x 5½", ceramic, circa 1960s, $110.00 – 125.00 (k) (notice Scotties around the base).

14", ceramic/plastic shade, marked "made in Japan," circa 1930s, $35.00 – 45.00 (p).

3½" x 12", pink flashed glass/metal, "Quin – puplets," Scotties on shade, circa 1930s, $300.00 – 375.00 (c).

3½" x 12", green flashed frosted glass/metal, "Quin – puplets," Scottie stenciled shade, circa 1930s, $175.00 – 225.00 (c).

12", pink and blue flashed frosted glass/metal, this is probably a marriage of two different colors, circa 1930s, $150.00 – 200.00 (p).

9", pink flashed glass/metal/plastic applied Scottie, circa 1930s, $80.00 – 100.00 (k).

11", frosted glass/metal, circa 1930s, $45.00 – 55.00 (p).

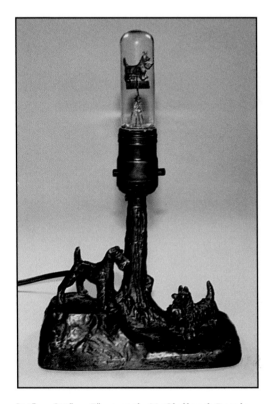

3½" x 6½" x 7", metal, McClellend Barclay, $150.00 – 180.00 (notice Scottie filament bulb), $50.00 – 75.00 (k).

3" x 3" x 4½", glass/metal, Scottie designs on shade are gone, circa 1930s, $45.00 – 55.00 (p).

4¾" x 2" x 8", metal, $60.00 – 85.00 (k).

5½" x 3" x 9", metal, $75.00 – 90.00 (k).

4¼" x 6¼" x 7", metal/glass, $100.00 – 120.00 (k).

5½" x 3" x 6", metal, $80.00 – 110.00 (k).

Planters

Planters are no doubt the most common Scottie items to be found in the marketplace. A person would have to have a very green thumb if all were used for their intended purpose.

5½" x 7½" x 3", ceramic, Napco, made in Japan, circa 1940s, $15.00 – 20.00 (p).

5½" x 7½" x 3", ceramic, Royal Haeger, made in USA, circa 1930s, $25.00 – 35.00 (p).

4" x 6" x 6", ceramic, circa 1950s, $25.00 – 35.00 (c).

4" x 2" x 2½", ceramic, circa 1950s, $10.00 – 20.00 (c).

4" x 1¼" x 1½", ceramic, marked "Hand painted in Occupied Japan," circa 1940s, $10.00 – 20.00 (c).

6" x 5" x 3", ceramic, $20.00 – 30.00 (c).

4" x 3½" x 3", made in Japan, circa 1940s, $15.00 – 20.00 (p).

4" x 5½", made in Japan, circa 1930s, $10.00 – 12.00 (p).

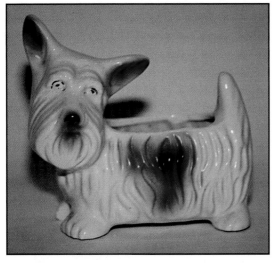

4" x 5½", made in Japan, circa 1940s, $10.00 – 12.00 (p).

5" x 4" x 2", made in Japan, circa 1940s, $10.00 – 12.00 (p).

3½" x 4½" x 2½", made in Japan, circa 1940s, $10.00 – 12.00 (p).

4½" x 2½" x 4", ceramic, Shawnee Pottery Co., USA, circa 1940s, $10.00 – 20.00 (p).

In this day and age, smoking does not inspire the clever accessories that it did earlier in the century. The fact that Scotties adorn vintage accessories may have been influenced by FDR's standard appearance with a cigarette and holder.

Ashtray, 9" x 2½", ceramic, $50.00 – 75.00 (k).

Ash Receiver, 2½" x 2" x 5", ceramic, Red Wing, circa 1930s, $250.00 – 350.00 (k).

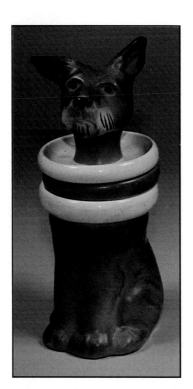

Cigarette Box, 3½" x 3½" x 1¼", plastic/metal, circa 1920s, $25.00 – 35.00 (p).

Cigarette Holder/Ashtray, 7" tall, porcelain, marked "Germany Goebel," $75.00 – 100.00 (c).

Ashtray, 10" x 6½" x 24", plaster, circa 1940s, $80.00 – 125.00 (c).

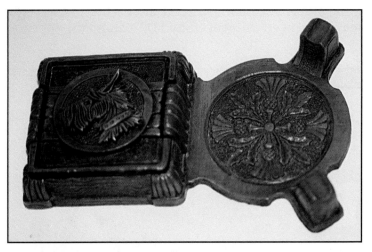

Cigarette Box/Ashtray, glass insert missing, 4" x 8" x 2", composition wood, SyrocoWood, circa 1940s, $20.00 – 24.00 (p).

Cigarette Box, 3¼" x 4" x 1¾", black amethyst glass/sterling silver overlay, Cambridge Glass Co., Cambridge, Ohio, circa 1930s, $175.00 – 225.00 (p).

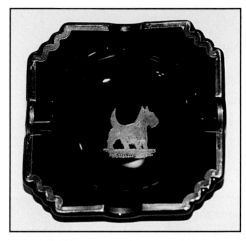

Ashtray, 5", black amethyst glass/sterling silver overlay, Cambridge Glass Co., Cambridge, Ohio, circa 1931 – 1934, $45.00 – 60.00 (c).

Ashtray, 4", black amethyst glass/sterling silver overlay, Fostoria Art Glass Co., Mayfair blank, circa 1930s, $50.00 – 75.00 (p).

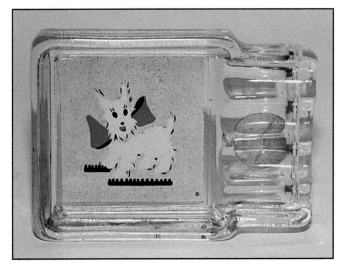

Ashtray, 3½" x 2½", glass/decal on reverse, sticker: Glass Art, Owens – Illinois, circa 1930s, $15.00 – 20.00 (p).

Ashtray, 6½" x 4" x 5", metal, circa 1930s, $25.00 – 50.00 (c).

Ashtray, 3½" x 3½" x 3", metal/copper wash, circa 1940s, $15.00 – 25.00 (c).

Ashtray, 6" x 6½" x 5", metal/bronze wash, circa 1940s, $25.00 – 40.00 (c).

Ashtray/Dish, 4¼" x 3¼", metal/bronze wash, Aberdeen terrier, $40.00 – 60.00 (k).

Ashtray, 6¼" x 5" x 3½", metal, $80.00 – 110.00 (k).

Ashtray, 6¼" x 5" x 3½", metal, $80.00 – 110.00 (k).

Picture at left shown open.

Ashtray/Calendar, 4" x 2½" x 4", metal, circa 1937, $25.00 – 40.00 (c).

Ashtray, 3" x 4", metal, marked "Japan," circa 1940s, $15.00 – 25.00 (c).

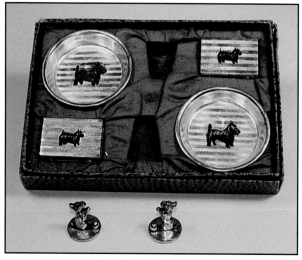

Smoke Set, metal/enamel, marked "Japan," circa 1940s, $75.00 – 100.00 (c).

Cigarette Holder/Match Safe, metal, circa 1930s, $25.00 – 40.00 (c).

Matchbox, 1¾" x 2½" x 1", cardboard/paper, made in Italy, history of Scottish Terrier on back, circa 1930s, $10.00 – 12.00 (p).

Match Striker, 2½" x 1½", cast iron, circa 1930s, $30.00 – 50.00 (k).

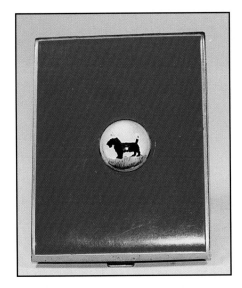

Cigarette Case, 3¾" x 2⅞", metal/intaglio reverse painted Scottie emblem, marked "WL6965," circa 1940s, $40.00 – 60.00 (c).

Cigarette Case, 3¾" x 3", gold tone metal/white enamel, $30.00 – 40.00 (k).

Cigarette Case, 3" x 3", metal, circa 1930s, $25.00 – 35.00 (k).

Cigarette Case, 2¼" x 3¼", metal, circa 1930s, $20.00 – 30.00 (k).

Cigarette Case, 3½" x 2½", metal, made in Japan, circa 1930s, $25.00 – 30.00 (p).

Automobile Cigarette Lighter, 2" x ¾", metal, circa 1950s, $50.00 – 75.00 (k).

Pipe Stand/Thermometer, 5" x 2½" x 2¾", metal, $75.00 – 90.00 (k).

Matchbook Cover, Superior Match Co., Chicago, Illinois, Bird's Eye View, Artist: Gil Elvgren, circa 1938, $5.00 – 12.00 (p).

Matchbook Cover, Lion Match Co., Inc., New York, New York, circa 1939, $5.00 – 10.00 (p).

Matchbook Cover, Diamond Match Co., New York City, circa 1930s, $5.00 – 10.00 (p).

Matchbook Covers, Diamond Match Co., New York City, circa 1930s, $5.00 – 10.00 each (p).

Matchbook Covers, left, Diamond Match Co., New York City; right, General Match Co., Cincinnati, Ohio, circa 1930s, $5.00 – 10.00 each (p).

Matchbook Covers, Diamond Match Co., New York City, circa 1930s, $5.00 – 10.00 each (p).

Statues

How could an artist choose a better subject than the stalwart Scottish Terrier? Posed regally or playfully, they are wonderfully distinctive models!

1½" x 5" x 3½", bone china, marked "HN1016," Royal Doulton, made in England, Champion Albourne Arthur, Designer: Frederick Daws, circa 1931 – 1985, $175.00 – 200.00 (c).

6½" x 3" x 6", china, marked "Made in England," Coopercraft North Staffordshire, $40.00 – 60.00 (c).

2" x 4" x 4", china, Styson, $10.00 – 20.00 (c).

5" x 3" x 4", porcelain, Lomonosov, Russia, L1059, circa 1990s, $25.00 – 50.00 (c).

3½" x 1¾" x 3½", porcelain, marked "Highbank Porcelain," Lochgilphead, Scotland, circa 1990s, $20.00 – 30.00 (c).

1¼" x 3" x 2½", china, Jock, sticker: "G Nov.Co. Japan," circa 1980s, $10.00 – 25.00 (c).

3½" x 4½", ceramic, made in Japan, circa 1930s, $7.00 – 10.00 (p).

4" x 5½", bone china, marked "Adderly, floral, Made in England," circa 1940s, $35.00 – 45.00 (p).

4¾" x 5¾" x 2¾", ceramic, made in Japan, circa 1940s, $10.00 – 15.00 (p).

3½" x 2¼" x 2¾", china, Wade, marked "Membership Special 1996/1997," circa 1996 – 1997, $40.00 – 60.00 (c).

6" x 12" x 6", ceramic, made in China, circa 1990s, $15.00 – 25.00 (c).

Pin, sent with above when joining the Wade Collectors Club, circa 1996 – 1997 (c).

5" x 1½" x 3¼", china, $30.00 – 50.00 (c).

4½" x 2" x 3½", pottery, sticker: "Toscany," made in Japan, circa 1990s, $10.00 – 20.00 (c).

7" x 4" x 5", Rosenthal, Germany, circa early 1900s, $275.00 – 350.00 (k).

2" x 3½" x 3", porcelain, John Joiner, Beatrix Potter, F. Warne & Co., 1990, Royal Albert, England, $40.00 – 60.00 (k).

Music Box, ceramic, Colter Designs, circa 1990s, $40.00 (c).

Music Box, 4" x 4", porcelain, Schmid, John Joiner, Beatrix Potter, circa 1980, $70.00 – 85.00 (k).

10" x 5" x 8", ceramic, Colter Designs, circa 1990s, $30.00 (c).

7" x 4" x 8", ceramic, Colter Designs, circa 1990s, $20.00 (c).

6¾", ceramic, made in Japan, Hummel imitation, circa 1940s, $10.00 – 12.00 (p).

"Begging His Share," 5½", china, Goebel Co., Germany, marked with full bee in V mark and has a hole in the cake, circa 1949 – 1959, $500.00 (p).

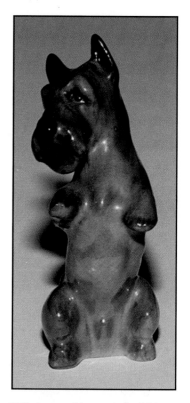

2¾", bone china, marked "Scottish Terrier, Royal Doulton, England, K10," circa 1931 – 1977, $150.00 – 175.00 (p).

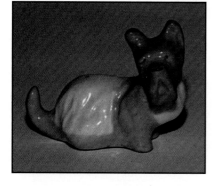

2¾" x 3¾", bone china, marked "Royal Worcester, V, Made in England, #2946," circa 1950s, $175.00 – 200.00 (p).

1½" x 1½", china, marked "Made in USSR," circa 1980s, $20.00 – 25.00 (p).

2¼", celluloid, made in Japan, circa 1930s, $15.00 – 25.00 (p).

3½" x 6" x 7", composition, circa 1990s, $10.00 – 25.00 (c).

1¼" x 2", composition, circa 1980s, $10.00 – 20.00 (c).

1½" x 3" x 3¼", coal/resin, $25.00 – 50.00 (c).

1½" x 1" x 3", composition, circa 1940s, $5.00 – 10.00 (c).

4" x 8" x 10", composition, circa 1990s, $20.00 – 30.00 (c).

4½" x 2¼", onyx, $5.00 – 10.00 (c).

3" x 1½" x 2¾", salt, $5.00 – 10.00 (c).

1½" x 3½" x 3", flocked plastic, circa 1950s, $5.00 –
10.00 (c).

2½" x 2½" x 4½", composition,
Possible Dreams International
Santa Collection, circa 1990s,
$10.00 – 25.00 (c).

"Snow Mom," 6½" x 4½" x 6", resin, made in China,
Lang and Wise Co., Delafield, Wisconsin, Artist: Sherry Buck Baldwin, circa 1990s, $38.00 (p).

"Holiday Carol," 5⅞" x 4½" x 5½", resin, made in China,
Lang and Wise Co., Delafield, Wisconsin, Artist: Sherry
Buck Baldwin, circa 1998, $60.00 (p).

2" x 2½", composition, made in England,
circa 1990s, $10.00 – 15.00 (c).

4" x 5" x 4", pottery, circa 1990s, $60.00 – 85.00 (k).

3" x 4", carnival chalkware, circa 1950s, $5.00 – 10.00 (p).

11" x 4" x 3½", carnival chalkware, circa 1930s, $35.00 – 50.00 (p).

10", carnival chalkware, circa 1930s, $55.00 – 75.00 (p).

9½" x 4" x 7", wax, circa 1990s, $25.00 – 35.00 (c).

4½" x 2" x 4", wax, circa 1990s, $5.00 – 15.00 (c).

JBs, glass by Boyd's Crystal Art Glass, left to right: Alpine Blue, Mint Green, Cobalt Carnival, Pocono Blue, Spring Surprise, Olympic White, prices vary depending on availability (c).

4½" x 1¾" x 3½", crystal, Baccarat, circa 1990s, $200.00 – 300.00 (k).

1½" x 4" x 3", blue carnival glass, marked "R.M. St. Clair, Elwood, Ind.," circa 1979, $150.00 – 200.00 (c).

1½" x 3" x 3", crystal, marked "Princess House Crystal Treasures, Germany," circa 1990s, $40.00 – 75.00 (c).

3½", glass, Heisey Glass Co., H89, Scottie Champ, circa 1941 – 1946, $150.00 – 175.00 (p).

3½", glass, Heisey by Imperial Glass Co., Scottie Champ, circa 1984, $65.00 – 85.00 (p).

1" x 3" x 3", glass, $10.00 – 25.00 (c).

2½", glass/composition, ME INK, Michel and Co., made in China, Artist: Mary Engelbreit, circa 1990s, $10.00 – 20.00 (c).

4", glass/wood/composition, circa 1997, $15.00 – 30.00 (c).

5¼" x 4", glass/composition, ME INK, Michel and Co., made in China, Artist: Mary Engelbreit, circa 1990s, $35.00 (p).

1¼" x 2¾" x 2", brass, circa 1980s, $5.00 – 15.00 (c).

6" x 2" x 4", cold cast bronze, DOGART by ED, circa 1990s, $60.00 – 75.00 (c).

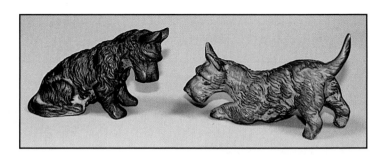

1½" x 3½" x 2", metal, circa 1940s, $20.00 – 40.00 (c).

6" x 2" x 4", cold cast bronze, Eden Valley Crafts, British artistry, $60.00 – 75.00 (c).

2" x 1", pewter, circa 1950s, $10.00 – 20.00 (c).

1" x 1" x 2¼", pewter, circa 1998, $25.00 – 50.00 (c).

2" x 1½" x 2", metal, circa 1940s, $7.00 – 15.00 (c).

2" x 4" x 3¾", lead, circa 1940s, $25.00 – 50.00 (c).

6½" x 3½" x 6¼", metal, marked "Vanio," circa 1935, $20.00 – 40.00 (c).

6" x 2" x 4½", metal, marked "Made in Japan," remainder of Canada souvenir sticker on side, circa 1940 – 1950s, $25.00 – 50.00 (c).

1½" x 2½" x 4¼", metal, circa 1940s, $15.00 – 25.00 (c).

3" x 1" x 2", metal, marked "J.B.," Jennings Brothers, circa 1920 – 1930s, $25.00 – 50.00 (c).

3" x 1" x 2", metal/copper wash, marked "Souvenir of Gettysburg, PA," circa 1940s, $20.00 – 35.00 (c).

2¼" x 1½" x 2¼", bronze, Austria, $80.00 – 110.00 (k).

2⅞" x 2" x 2⅞", bronze, Asprey, circa 1950, $300.00 – 350.00 (k).

3½" x 1½" x 1", bronze, marked "Gorham, MK or M. Kirmse," circa 1920 – 1930s, $500.00 – 800.00 (k) (originally sold for about two pounds sterling).

3½" x 1½" x 2", bronze, marked "Gorham, MK or M. Kirmse," circa 1920 – 1930s, $500.00 – 800.00 (k) (originally sold for about two pounds sterling).

3½" x 1½ x 2", bronze, marked "Gorham, MK or M. Kirmse," circa 1920 – 1930s, $1,200.00 – 1,500.00 (k) (originally sold for about two pounds sterling).

4½" x 2" x 3½", bronze, circa 1950s, $180.00 – 200.00 (k).

2", cast iron, circa 1930s, $50.00 – 60.00 (p).

2" x ¾" x 1¾", wood, $20.00 – 40.00 (c).

1½" x 4½" x 4", wood, $20.00 – 40.00 (c).

Merry Christmas, try your luck, row a boat, feed the baby. What do these phrases have in common? Scotties of course!

Christmas Ornaments, porcelain, Artist: Mary Engelbreit, set of six, circa 1998, $38.00 – 45.00 (c).

Christmas Ornament, composition, Enesco, circa 1980s, $15.00 – 25.00 (c).

Christmas Ornament, composition, circa 1990s, $5.00 – 10.00 (c).

Christmas Ornament, composition, Artist: Sherry Buck Baldwin, circa 1998, $10.00 – 15.00 (c).

Christmas Ornament, composition, circa 1990s, $8.00 – 15.00 (c).

Christmas Ornament, ceramic, circa 1996, $15.00 – 25.00 (c).

Christmas Light Bulb, 3",
glass/metal, Japan, circa
1930s, $60.00 – 90.00 (k).

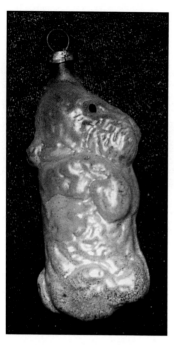

Christmas Ornament, glass, circa
1920s, $150.00 – 180.00 (k).

Christmas Ornament, pewter, marked "Seagull
Pewter Canada," circa 1990s, $15.00 – 25.00
(c).

Christmas Ornament, metal, circa 1990s,
$15.00 – 25.00 (c).

Christmas Ornament, pewter, circa 1998,
$10.00 – 20.00 (c).

Door Knob Ornament, leather/metal,
circa 1990s, $10.00 – 20.00 (c).

Lamp Finial, composition/metal, circa 1990s, $8.00 – 12.00 (c).

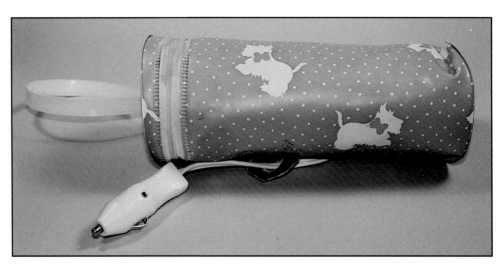

Baby Bottle Warmer, plastic, Gerber, circa 1990s, $10.00 – 20.00 (c).

Magnet, 1½" x 2¼", paper/metal/plastic, circa 1990s, $5.00 – 7.00 (p).

Magnets, 3", composition, circa 1990s, $5.00 – 10.00 each (c).

Eyeglasses, 7½" across, Bakelite, Anglo-American Eye Wear, England, circa 1980s, $225.00 – 275.00 (k).

Sign, 10", plastic, circa 1990s, $5.00 – 15.00 (c).

Shade Pulls, 1½" x 1 5/8", celluloid, circa 1930s, $5.00 – 10.00 each (p).

Printer's Block, 3½" x 3¾", wood/metal, "Use Christmas Seals - fight emphysema, air pollution, tuberculosis, 1974 Christmas Greetings," $40.00 – 60.00 (k).

Wall Hook, 3" x 5", pewter, circa 1990s, $15.00 – 25.00 (c).

Fabric Cutters, metal, circa 1930s, $100.00 – 120.00 and $150.00 – 180.00 (k).

Steering Wheel Knob, 1½" x 2½", Bakelite/reverse painted glass/ chrome, circa 1940s, $80.00 – 120.00 (k).

Door Knocker, 5½" x 4", brass, made in England, circa 1940s, $100.00 – 125.00 (p).

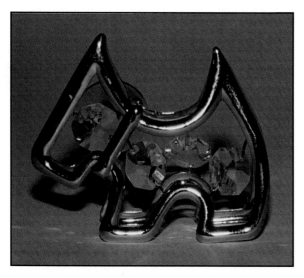

Sun Catcher, 3" x 2½", plastic/metal, made in China, circa 1990s, $5.00 – 7.00 (p).

Dog Dish Holder, 8½" x 8½" x 6", cast iron, Hubley No. 350, circa 1940s, $100.00 – 150.00 (p).

Hand Wrought Fireplace Screen, metal, $300.00 – 350.00 (k).

Fireplace Grate, 19" x 12" x 16", cast iron, Werner Foundry Inc., Koppers Coke, Lansdale, Pennsylvania, $600.00 – 700.00 (k).

Fence Post Top, 12", cast iron/threaded inside, $400.00 – 600.00 (k).

Paddle, wood, circa 1950s, $100.00 – 120.00 (k).

Massager, 6" x 3" x 4½", wood, circa 1990s, $10.00 – 20.00 (c).

Punch Board, 13" x 5" x 16", paper; Scotties, 2½ x 3" x 1", metal, $180.00 – 225.00 (k).

Leash Holder, 17" x 7", composition wood, circa 1990s, $25.00 (p).

Punch Board with the Scottie you could win, $50.00 – 70.00 (board only) (k).

Kitchen and Entertaining

Scotties are very entertaining canines to live with, so it makes sense to have them represented on the tools you use in the kitchen and at parties.

Salt and Pepper Shakers, 3", ceramic, made in Japan, circa early 1900s, $15.00 – 20.00 (p).

Salt and Pepper Shakers, 1¼" x 3" x 2½", ceramic, circa 1980s, $20.00 – 30.00 (c).

Salt and Pepper Shakers, 1½" x 1½" x 2¾", ceramic, circa 1950s, $10.00 – 20.00 (c).

Salt and Pepper Shakers, 2¼", ceramic, made in China, circa 1980s, $12.00 – 15.00 (p).

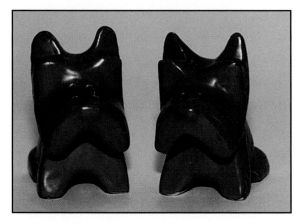

Salt and Pepper Shakers, 3", ceramic, sticker: Tudor Potteries, Hollywood Ware, Los Angeles, California, circa 1930s, $35.00 – 45.00 (p).

Salt and Pepper Shakers in original carrying tray, 4½" x 3¼", milk glass/metal, Tipp City, Ohio, USA, circa 1940s, $45.00 – 65.00 set (p).

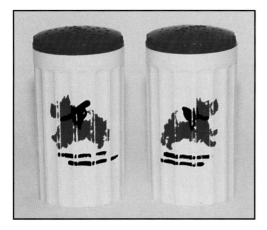

Salt and Pepper Shakers, 3¼", plastic, marked "Richelain," circa 1940s, $10.00 – 15.00 (p).

Salt and Pepper Shakers, 3¼", ceramic, circa 1990s, $15.00 – 18.00 (p).

Salt and Pepper Shakers, ceramic, made in China, circa 1990s, $10.00 – 15.00 (c).

Sugar and Creamer, 3¼", ceramic, Morton Potteries, Morton, Illinois, patterned after Grape Nuts creamer of the late 1930s, brown, circa 1940s, $15.00 – 25.00 each (p).

Sugar, 3¼", ceramic, Morton Potteries, Morton, Illinois, patterned after Grape Nuts creamer of the late 1930s, black, circa 1940s, $15.00 – 25.00 each (p).

Creamer, 3¼", ceramic, Morton Potteries, Morton, Illinois, patterned after Grape Nuts creamer of the late 1930s, dark blue, circa 1940s, $15.00 – 25.00 each (p).

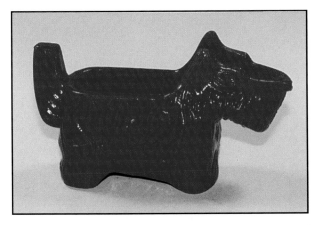

Creamer, red slag glass, thought to be "end of the day" piece done by L.E. Smith with the Grape Nuts creamer mold, $20.00 – 30.00 (k).

Mug, ceramic, Artist: Edwin Megargee, circa 1940s, $20.00 – 40.00 (c).

Mugs, ceramic, Lady and The Tramp, Disney, circa 1990s, $6.00 – 12.00 (c).

Mug, 4", ceramic, ME INK, Kansas City, Missouri, made in Taiwan, Artist: Mary Engelbreit, circa 1992, $10.00 (p).

Mugs, ceramic, circa 1990s, $8.00 – 15.00 each (c).

Mug, 4", ceramic, made in Mexico, Ferrioni, circa 1990s, $15.00 (p).

Child's Mug, 3¾", milk glass, Hazel Atlas Glass Co., circa 1930s, $30.00 – 50.00 (p).

Sherbet, 3½", milk glass, circa 1930s, $20.00 – 25.00 (p).

Sugar and Creamer, 3½", Twas the Night Before Christmas, china, made in Indonesia by Noritake, circa 1990s, $25.00 – 35.00 per set (p).

Teapot, Twas the Night Before Christmas, 5½" x 7" x 4", ceramic, made in China, designed for Noritake, circa 1990s, $55.00 – 65.00 (p).

Candy Dish, left, 6½" x 6½", Napkin Holder, right, 4½" x 4½" x 3¼", Twas the Night Before Christmas, ceramic, made in China, designed for Noritake, circa 1990s, $25.00 – 35.00 each (p).

Teapot, 3½" x 7" x 7", ceramic, Japan, circa 1930s, $75.00 – 100.00 (k).

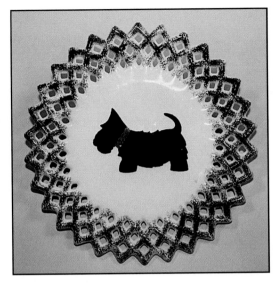

Decorative Plate, ceramic, Colter Designs, circa 1990s, $20.00 (c).

Pie Bird, 4½", pottery, made in England, circa early 1900s, $200.00 – 225.00 (p).

Dish, 4", porcelain, Highbank Porcelain, Lochgilphead, Scotland, circa 1990s, $15.00 – 25.00 (c).

Votive Candle Holder, 3½", made in China, circa 1980s, $5.00 – 7.00 (p).

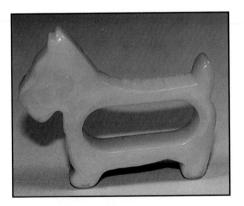

Napkin Ring, Bakelite, circa 1940s, $45.00 – 100.00 (c).

Napkin Ring, Bakelite, circa 1940s, $45.00 – 100.00 (c).

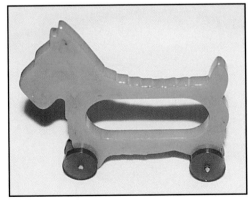

Napkin Ring, Bakelite, circa 1940s, $60.00 – 125.00 (c).

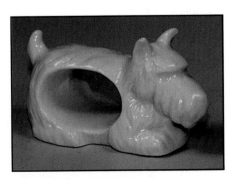

Napkin Ring, 1½" x 3½" x 2", ceramic, $8.00 – 15.00 (c).

Napkin Rings, metal, circa 1990s, $25.00 – 35.00 set (c).

Napkin Ring, 2" x 3", wood, circa
1950s, $40.00 – 50.00 (k).

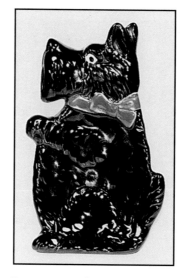

Tile, 6" x 6", ceramic, marked "Soriano Ceram-
ics," circa 1980s, $20.00 – 30.00 (c).

Spoon Rest, 3" x 5½", ceramic,
circa 1990s, $10.00 – 20.00 (c).

String Holder, 3½" x 3" x 6", ceramic,
made in Japan, circa 1930s, $60.00 –
90.00 (k).

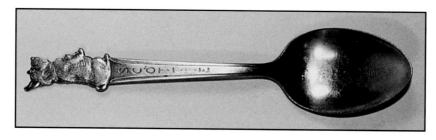

Spoon, 5", silverplated, circa 1940s, $10.00 – 20.00 (c).

Party Favor, plastic, circa 1950s, $3.00 – 10.00 (c).

Spoons, 1" x 5", plastic, marked "Beetleware 9576," (c). P.L. Crosby, circa 1933, $15.00 – 30.00 each. Colors shown: red, yellow, blue, green, and orange. Note: originally came with a bowl featuring the "Skippy" cartoon character.

Bar Tool, Cocktail Recipes, 3" x 1" x 2½", Bakelite, circa 1930 – 1940s, $90.00 – 120.00 (k).

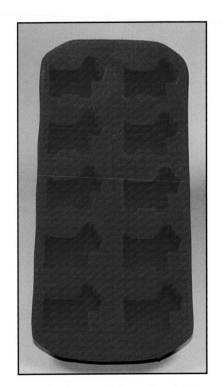

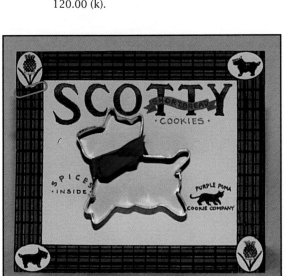

Ice Cube Tray, rubber, circa 1990s, $8.00 – 15.00 (c).

Cookie Cutter, 2½" x 2½", aluminum, Purple Puma Cookie Co., circa 1990s, $12.00 (p).

Coasters, 3", metal, circa 1940s, $10.00 – 15.00 each (c).

Coaster Set, 7" x 5" x 7", wood, circa 1980s, $20.00 – 30.00 (c).

Coaster, rubber, circa 1990s, $1.00 – 3.00 (c).

Coasters, 4½" x 4½", tile/cork, Highland Graphics Inc., Faithful Companion, Artist: Debbie Mum, circa 1990s, $15.00 (p).

Ice Bucket, 12" x 7½" x 7½", plastic/cardboard, marked "Donde," circa 1980s, $25.00 – 35.00 (p).

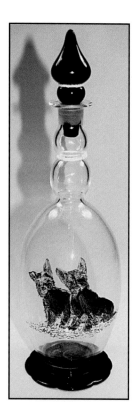

Decanter, 9", etched glass, circa 1930s, $100.00 – 120.00 (k).

Tumbler, 5¾", glass/copper band, circa 1950s, $50.00 – 80.00 (p).

Tumblers, 4½", glass, circa 1940s, $8.00 – 18.00 each (p).

Tumbler, 5½", glass, "Three Canny Scots" decoration, Cambridge Glass Co., circa 1930s, $50.00 – 80.00 (p).

Tumblers, 4¾", glass, circa 1930s, $8.00 – 18.00 each (p).

Tumbler, 4½", glass, Hazel Atlas Glass Co., circa 1930s, $8.00 – 18.00 (p).

Tumbler, 4½", glass, circa 1930s, $8.00 – 18.00 (p).

Tumbler, 4½", glass, Hazel Atlas
Glass Co., circa 1930s, $8.00 –
18.00 (p).

Tumbler, 6½", glass, circa 1930s,
$12.00 – 20.00 (p).

Tumbler, 4½", glass, Libbey,
circa 1930s, $8.00 – 18.00 (p).

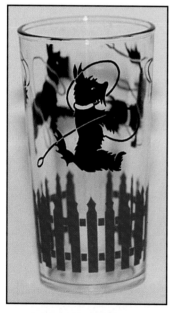

Tumbler, 5", glass, Hazel Atlas
Glass Co., circa 1930s, $8.00 –
18.00 (p).

Tumbler, 3½", glass, Federal
Glass Co., circa 1950s, $8.00 –
15.00 (c).

Tumbler, 6", glass, $15.00 –
20.00 (c).

Shot Glass, 2¼", circa 1950s, $8.00 – 15.00 (c).

Tumbler, 4", and Swizzle Stick, 6½", glass/ceramic Scotties, circa 1980s, $15.00 – 20.00 per set (p).

Tumbler, 7", decorated frosted glass, Libbey, circa 1930s, $12.00 – 20.00 (p).

Salt, 4" x 2½", etched crystal, circa 1940s, $20.00 – 35.00 (c).

Salt, 2½", etched crystal, circa 1940s, $15.00 – 25.00 (c).

Candy Dish, 5½" x 5½" x 1", crystal glass/frosted, embossed Scotties, reminiscent of Meta Pluckebaum's Sandy and Jock, circa 1940s, $20.00 – 25.00 (p).

Child's Plate, 5½" x 5½", Jade-ite glass, circa 1930s, Laurel by McKee Glass Company, $75.00 – 100.00 (p).

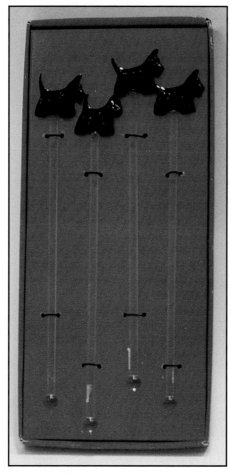

Place Card Holder, 1½" x ½" x 1½", cast iron, Hubley No. 439, circa 1940s, $35.00 – 60.00 (c).

Swizzle Stick, 6", glass/pewter, $10.00 – 15.00 (c).

Swizzle Sticks, 7", plastic, circa 1980s, $20.00 – 25.00 set (p).

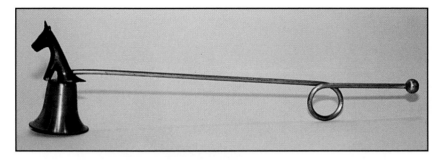

Candle Snuffer, 9" x 2½", brass/pot metal, circa 1920s, $45.00 – 55.00 (p).

Tea Bag Holder, made in England, circa 1940s, $30.00 – 35.00 (p).

Canisters, 4¼", 5", 5½", tin, Artist: S. Buck Baldwin, circa 1996, $10.00 – 20.00 per set (c).

Canisters, 5½", 6", 6½", tin, circa 1950s, $35.00 – 50.00 per set (p).

Cake Carrier, 11" x 10", tin, circa 1950s, $35.00 – 55.00 (p).

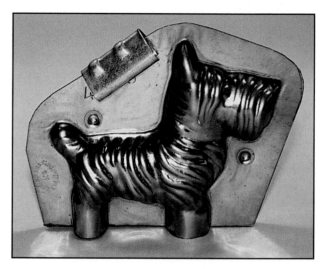

Chocolate Mold, 6½" x 2" x 5", tin, Anton Riche, $125.00 – 150.00 (k).

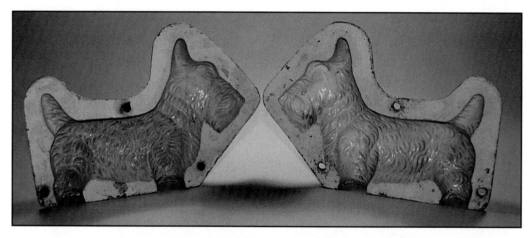

Ice Cream Mold, 8" x 2" x 6", metal, circa 1950s, $125.00 – 150.00 (k).

Chocolate Mold, 5½" x 1½" x 5", tin, marked "383," $125.00 – 150.00 (k).

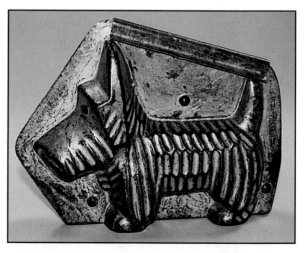

Chocolate Mold, 4" x 1½" x 3½", tin, marked "4978 Letang Fils 108," $125.00 – 150.00 (k).

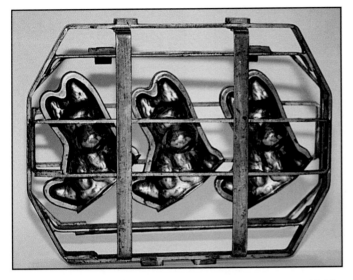

Dish, 3" x 4½", metal, circa 1940s, $15.00 – 25.00 (c).

Chocolate Mold, 12" x 9" x 2½", tin/cast iron, circa 1940s, marked "2753," $125.00 – 150.00 (p).

Dish, 4", aluminum, $45.00 – 65.00 (c).

Tin, 5⅝" x 3⅞" x 2½", tin, Artist: Mary Engelbreit, circa 1990s, $15.00 – 20.00 (p).

Bottle Stopper, carved, open position, circa 1940s, $75.00 – 125.00 (c).

Bottle Stopper, carved, closed position, circa 1940s, $75.00 – 125.00 (c).

Corkscrew, 4" x 1" x 3", wood/metal, circa 1950s, $15.00 – 25.00 (c).

Napkin Holder, 5½" x 6¼" x 3¾", pine, circa 1930s, $18.00 – 22.00 (p).

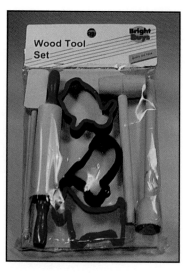

Child's Baking Set, wood/plastic, circa 1990s, $5.00 – 15.00 (c).

Napkin Holder, 5½" x 3" x 5", wood, circa 1950s, $10.00 – 25.00 (c).

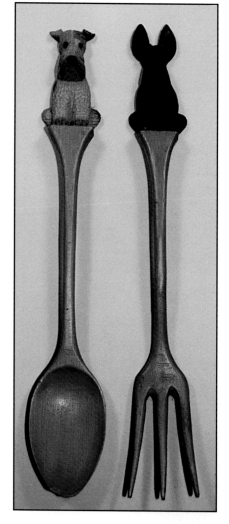

Salad Set, 1¾" x 11", wood, $60.00 – 80.00 (k).

Paper Napkin, England, circa 1990s, $1.00 – 3.00 (c).

Bedroom and Bathroom

From the delicate feminine powder jars to the sturdy masculine tie racks, Scotties are definitely fixtures in the bedroom and bathroom.

Perfume Solid, 2" x ¾" x 1½", enameled metal, Estee Lauder, circa 1990s, $75.00 – 100.00 (c).

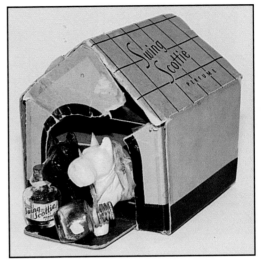

Perfume, "Swing Scottie," 4" x 3¾" x 3", cardboard box/celluloid Scotties/glass bottles, Quality Products Co., Le Centre, Minnesota, circa 1936, $25.00 – 35.00 (p).

Perfume, 3½" x 2¼", celluloid dog/ribbon/glass bottle, Dreams Rose Perfume, made in Japan, circa 1930s, $12.00 – 15.00 (p).

Purse Mirror, 3" x 2½", glass, circa 1940s, $40.00 – 60.00 (c).

Trinket Box, 2" x 1½" x 2", porcelain, Limoges, France, circa 1990s, $90.00 – 120.00 (k).

Trinket Box, 2¾" x 1¾" x 3¾", porcelain, circa 1997, $20.00 – 40.00 (c).

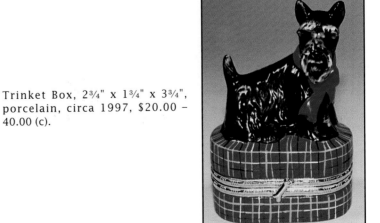

Trinket Box, 2" x 2" x 2", porcelain, circa 1990s, $10.00 – 30.00 (c).

Powder Jar, 4½" x 5½", glass, My Pet, Diamond Glass Co., circa 1930s, $85.00 – 125.00 (p).

Powder Jar, opaque pink, 3½" x 6½", glass, circa 1930 – 1940s, Akro Agate, marked "Made in US of America," with Akro Agate symbol, a crow flying through an A carrying marbles in its beak and claws, $150.00 – 200.00 (c).

Powder Jar, opaque blue, 3½" x 6½", glass, circa 1930 – 1940s, Akro Agate, marked "Made in US of America," with Akro Agate symbol, a crow flying through an A carrying marbles in its beak and claws, $150.00 – 200.00 (c).

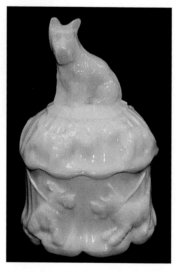

Powder Jar, opaque white, 3½" x 6½", glass, circa 1930 – 1940s, Akro Agate, marked "Made in US of America," with Akro Agate symbol, a crow flying through an A carrying marbles in its beak and claws, $150.00 – 200.00 (c).

Jar, 2½" x 4", glass, marked "Des. Pat 107082," $25.00 – 50.00 (c).

Toothbrush Holder, 2½" x 1½" x 2", ceramic, Mission B.C., circa 1980s, $15.00 – 30.00 (k).

Pitcher and Bowl, ceramic, Colter Designs, circa 1990s, $100.00 (c).

Brush, 5½" x 2" x 3½", wood, circa 1940s, $25.00 – 50.00 (c).

Guest Towels, paper, circa 1950s, $5.00 – 7.00 per towel (c).

Towel Rack, 12" x 5¾, wood, circa 1930s, $25.00 – 30.00 (p).

Towel Rack, 12" x 5¾", wood, circa 1930s,
$25.00 – 30.00 (k).

Towel Rack, 13" x 8", fabric/embroidered,
circa 1950s, $80.00 – 100.00 (k).

Soap, circa 1990s, $5.00 – 10.00 set (c).

Tie Rack, 9½" x 6" x 4½", composition wood/metal, circa 1930s,
$35.00 – 50.00 (p).

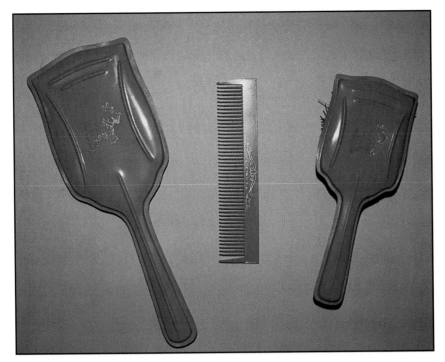

Child's Vanity Set, plastic, circa 1940s, $25.00 – 50.00 (c).

Hat Stand, 3¼" x 3¼" x ½", wood/glass, circa 1920s, $50.00 – 75.00 (k).

Hatbox, 7½" x 11½", paper, Stetson Millinery, $80.00 – 95.00 (k).

Hanger, 16½" x 12", wood, marked "Stupell Johnston, RI USA," circa 1990s, $15.00 – 20.00 (c).

Jewelry and Accessories

Wherever they adorn, Scotties will be noticed.

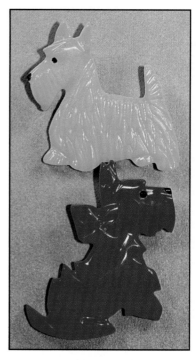

Pins, old Bakelite/new carvings, Ron and Ester Shultz, $75.00 – 125.00 each (c).

Pins, old Bakelite/new carvings, Ron and Ester Shultz, $125.00 – 200.00 each (c).

Pins, Bakelite, circa 1940s, $50.00 – 100.00 each (c).

Pins, Bakelite, circa 1940s, $50.00 – 100.00 each (c).

Pins, plastic, circa 1940s, $15.00 – 25.00 each (c).

Pins, plastic, circa 1940s, $15.00 – 25.00 each (c).

Pin, 1¾" x 1¼", plastic, 1950s, $15.00 – 25.00 (p).

Pin, 4" x 1", celluloid, sweater pin, circa 1930s, $22.00 – 25.00 (p).

Pin, 2¾" x 2¼", plastic/metal, AB Originals, circa 1993, $10.00 (p).

Pins, metal, circa 1990s, $5.00 – 15.00 each (c).

Pin, sterling silver, Artist: Mary Engelbreit, circa 1990s, issue price $25.00 (c).

Pin, metal, circa 1940s, $10.00 – 15.00 (c).

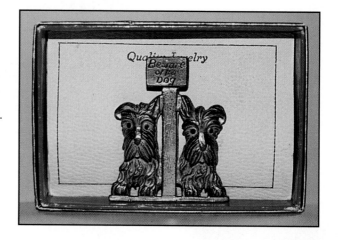

Pins, metal, circa 1990s, $10.00 – 20.00 each (c).

Pins, sterling silver, circa 1990s, $25.00 – 40.00 each (c).

Pins, metal, circa 1990s, $5.00 – 15.00 each (c).

Pin, 2½", sterling silver, circa 1950s, $20.00 – 30.00 (p).

Pins, metal, circa 1950s (center 1990s), $10.00 – 20.00 each (c).

Pin, 3½", gold tone metal, circa 1990s, $10.00 (p).

Pin, 2" x 1¾", sterling silver, casting of antique celluloid pin, Tartan Terrier, circa 1990s, $35.00 (p).

Pin, 1", gold tone metal/faux pearl, circa 1940s, $10.00 – 15.00 (p).

Pin, 1½" x 1¾", gold tone metal/enamel, circa 1990s, $10.00 – 15.00 (p).

Pins, wood, circa 1940s, $25.00 – 30.00 each (k).

Pin, 2" x 1½", clay/metal, Creations From the Heart, Artist: Debbie Miller, circa 1990s, $8.00 – 12.00 (p).

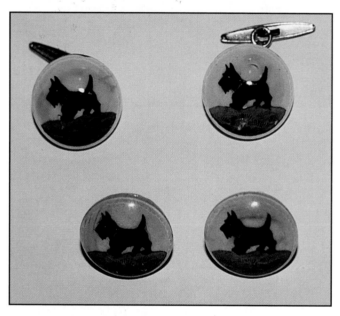

Cufflinks and Earrings, sterling/glass/reverse painted on glass, circa 1930s, $35.00 – 50.00 each (p).

Earrings and Pendant, gold tone metal/plastic, marked "SJC," circa 1980s, $10.00 – 12.00 set (p).

Shoulder Bag Pin, gold tone metal, circa 1950s, $15.00 – 25.00 (c).

Charm, sterling silver, circa 1990s, $15.00 – 25.00 (c).

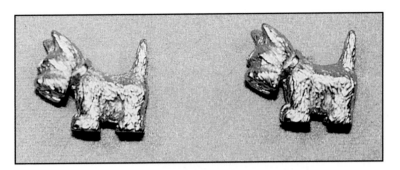

Cuff Links, circa 1950s, $25.00 – 40.00 (c).

Watch, circa 1990s,
$20.00 – 40.00 (c).

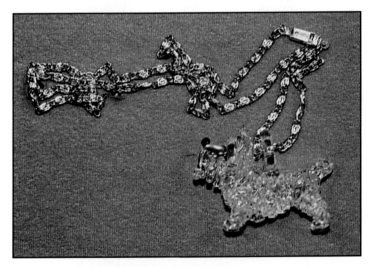

Charm Bracelet, 8", sterling silver, circa 1990s, $85.00 –
125.00 (p).

Necklace, glass, $10.00 – 15.00 (c).

Tie Clasp, circa 1950s, $10.00 – 15.00 (c).

Bracelets, metal, $80.00 – 90.00 each (k).

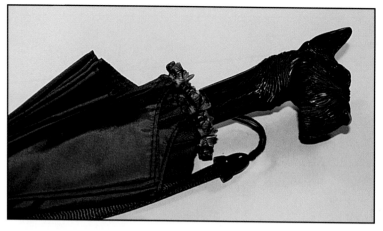

Puzzle Key Ring, plastic, circa 1940s, $15.00 – 25.00 (c).

Umbrella, wood, circa 1940s, $300.00 – 350.00 (k) (notice the tips of the umbrella staves).

Key Ring, metal, circa 1990s, current $5.00 – 10.00 (c).

Belt Buckle, composition, circa 1940s, $10.00 – 20.00 (c).

Compact, 3½" x 2", silk top/gold tone metal, $20.00 – 30.00 (k).

Compact, 3¼", gold tone metal, $20.00 – 30.00 (k).

Compact, 3", metal/marcasite/enamel, $40.00 – 50.00 (k).

Compact, 3" x 3", wood/metal, $30.00 – 35.00 (k).

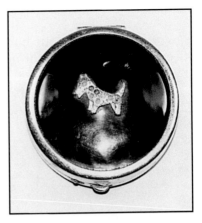

Compact, 2", metal/marcasite/enamel, $35.00 – 45.00 (k).

Child's Purse, vinyl, circa 1950s, $10.00 – 20.00 (c).

Purse, 13" x 11" x 4", plastic/metal/wool/rayon/acetate, Garay, circa 1930s, $85.00 – 100.00 (p).

Purse, plastic/cotton crocheted bag, circa 1940s, $150.00 – 200.00 (c).

Amulet Purse, glass beads/metal charms/cotton, Tartan Terrier, circa 1990s, $45.00 – 55.00 (c).

Textiles

Cover your floors, your body, and your walls, because Scotties are plentiful in wool, cotton, and silk. This section also has a bit of nepotism. Candee is a very proud Nana, and Patty is a very proud "honorary aunt."

Pin Cushion, 1" x 1½" x 1", pewter, England, circa 1990s, $25.00 – 40.00 (c).

Tape Measure, 1½" x 1", metal/satin, Germany, circa 1940s, $40.00 – 60.00 (c).

Thimble, 1", sterling silver, Tartan Terrier, circa 1990s, $25.00 – 40.00 (c).

Pin Cushion, 5" x 5" x 3", silk/composition wood/lace/sawdust, circa 1940s, Japan, $15.00 – 25.00 (p).

Hooked Rug, wool, circa 1930s, $150.00 – 200.00 (c).

Hooked Rug, wool, circa 1940s, $100.00 – 150.00 (c).

Hooked Rug, wool, circa 1938, $200.00 – 250.00 (k).

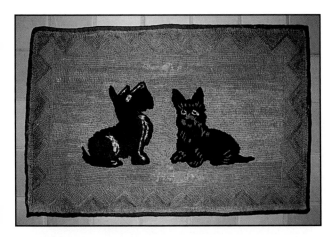

Hooked Rug, wool, circa 1940s, $300.00 – 350.00 (k).

Hooked Rug, wool, circa 1960s, $200.00 – 250.00 (k).

Hooked Rug, wool, circa 1940s, $100.00 – 150.00 (c).

Hooked Chair Pad, wool, circa 1950s, $60.00 – 80.00 (k).

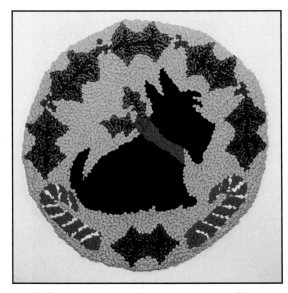

Hooked Chair Pad, wool, Angus Stitches, made by Candee Davis, circa 1990s (c).

Hooked Rug, wool, Angus Stitches, made by Candee Davis, circa 1990s (c).

Hooked Rug, wool, Angus Stitches, made by Candee Davis, circa 1990s (c).

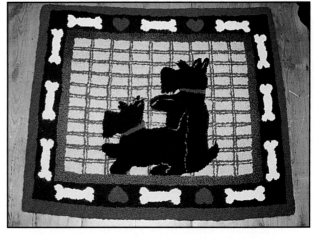

Hooked Rug, wool, Angus Stitches, made by Candee Davis, circa 1990s (c).

Hooked Rug, wool, Angus Stitches, made by Candee Davis, circa 1990s (c).

Hooked Rug, wool, made by Jean Michel Dumas, circa 1995, $100.00 – 120.00 (k).

Rug, linoleum, circa 1940s, $200.00 – 250.00 (k).

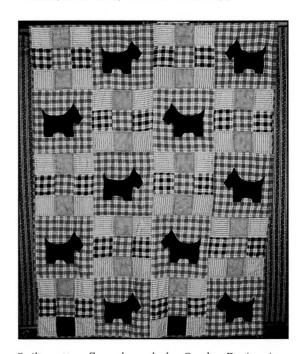

Quilt, cotton flannel, made by Candee Davis, circa 1997 (c).

Quilt, cotton flannel, made by Candee Davis, circa 1998 (c).

Throw, woven acrylic, Beacon Manufacturing Co., circa 1997, $30.00 – 50.00 (c).

Baby Blanket, cotton, Stevens, circa 1940s, $50.00 – 75.00 (c).

Machine Lace, cotton, $5.00 – 15.00 (c).

Tablecloth and Napkins, linen, circa 1940s, $30.00 – 60.00 set (c).

Handkerchief Box, 8¼" x 8¼", cardboard, circa 1940s, $10.00 – 20.00 (c).

Handkerchief Box, 8¼" x 8¼", cardboard, circa 1940s, $10.00 – 20.00 (p).

Handkerchief, cotton, circa 1940s, $10.00 – 20.00 (c).

Handkerchief, cotton, circa 1940s, $10.00 – 20.00 (c).

Handkerchief, cotton, circa 1940s, $10.00 – 20.00 (c).

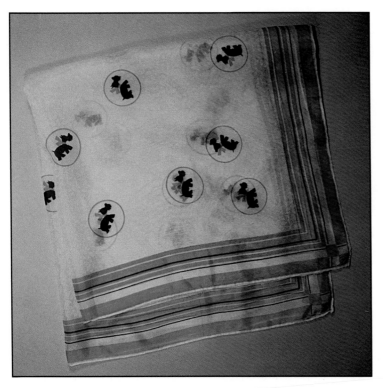

Scarf, silk, circa 1950s, $20.00 – 40.00 (c).

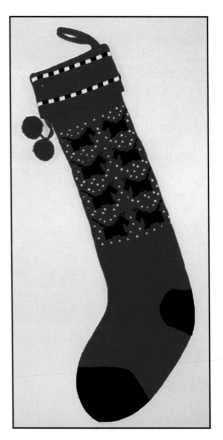

Christmas Stocking, acrylic yarn, circa 1980s, $15.00 – 30.00 (c).

Christmas Stocking, wool, needlepoint, circa 1990s, $25.00 – 30.00 (c).

Sewing Patterns, circa 1980s, $5.00 – 10.00 (c).

Dish Towel, cotton, hand embroidered, circa 1940s, $10.00 – 12.00 (p).

Embroidery transfers, circa 1990s (reprint), $2.00 – 5.00 (c).

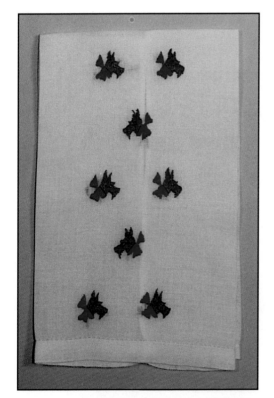

Towel, linen, circa 1950s, $5.00 – 10.00 (c).

Towel, linen, circa 1940s, $5.00 – 10.00 (c).

Towel Set, terry cloth, circa 1990s, $10.00 – 15.00 (p).

Needlepoint Pillow, wool, circa 1997, $40.00 – 60.00 (c).

Needlepoint Picture, wool, circa 1940s, $20.00 – 25.00 (c).

Needlepoint Picture, 8" x 10", wool, circa 1940s, $25.00 – 30.00 (p).

Cross-stitched Pillow, cotton, circa 1980s, $25.00 – 50.00 (c).

Cross-stitched Pillow, cotton, circa 1980s, $25.00 – 50.00 (c).

Cross-stitch Designs adapted from vintage silhouettes, Angus Stitches, circa 1998 (c).

Embroidered Sampler, cotton, circa 1940s, $25.00 – 50.00 (c).

Candee Davis's grandchild, Courtney Moriah, 5, modeling a few examples of Scottie textiles available in 1998 (c).

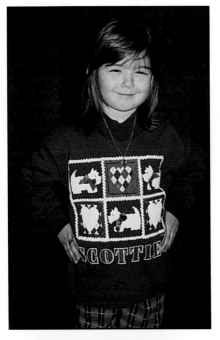

Candee Davis's grandchildren, Courtney Moriah, 5, and Nicholas Tyler, 2½, modeling a few examples of Scottie textiles available in 1998 (c).

Candee Davis's parents, Virginia and Martin Sten, who met because of two Scotties. They will soon celebrate their 62nd anniversary. Pictured with their great-grandchildren, Courtney and Nicholas (c).

Candee Davis's son, Joshua, and daughter-in-law, Tammee, with two of their three furry family members, Shadow and Mittens. Jasmine was camera-shy (c).

Candee Davis's daughter, Colleen, and her son, Nicholas (c).

Rothmoor Coat Charm, 1" x ¾", gold tone metal, marked "Genuine Rothmoor Coat," circa 1940s, $15.00 – 20.00 (p).

Candee Davis's son-in-law, Jeremy (c).

Martha Jean Ade, daughter of Patty's photographer for Volume I, Sharon Ade and her doctor, David Ade. She is the fifth of six children, shown here at age 9 (p).

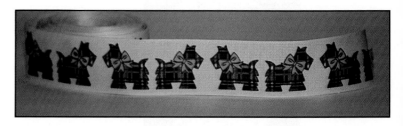

Ribbon, 1½" wide, acrylic, circa 1900s, $2.25 per yard (p).

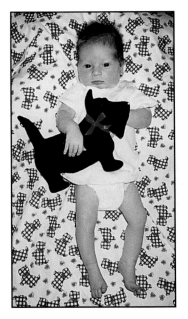

Buttons, ⅝", celluloid on original paper card, Le Chic, made in USA, original price tag of 10¢ is on back of card, circa 1930s, $12.00 for complete card (p).

Mary Therese Ade, daughter of Patty Baugh's photographer for Volume I, Sharon Ade, and her doctor, David Ade. Born July 4, 1998, the youngest of six. Shown here at ages five days and four months (p).

Children's Hangers, plastic, $5.00 – 10.00 each (c).

A wide variety of buttons spanning 60 years of Scottie fasteners. Materials include plastic, celluloid, Bakelite, ceramic, metal, and wood. Prices range from $1.00 to $30.00 depending on material, age, and availability (c).

Ribbon, 1½" x 2½", flocked Scotties, taffeta and wire, circa 1990s, $3.00 – 5.00 per yard (p).

Printed Material

Calendars and Advertisements

A Scottish terrier is handsome, strong, endearing, trustworthy, and loyal. Those qualities have made him the perfect spokesman for many products through the years.

Calendars, 5½" x 4", 3½" x 3¾", 2½" x 3", metal/paper, circa 1941, $30.00 – 50.00 each (k).

Calendar, paper, circa 1939, $40.00 – 50.00 (k).

Calendar, 6" x 4", paper/metal, gift from R. R. Mittelbusher and Vern B. Hartung Insurance, Davenport, Iowa, circa 1943, $15.00 – 20.00 (p).

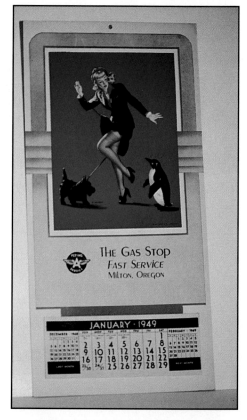

Calendar, 6" x 15", paper, gift from The Gas Stop in Milton, Oregon, Artist: Elvgren, circa 1949, $20.00 – 25.00 (p).

Calendar Holder, 8" x 17", embossed paper, calendar missing, circa 1940 – 1970s, $35.00 – 50.00 (with or without calendar) (p).

Calendar, circa 1999, $10.00 – 15.00 (c).

Calendar, circa 1989, $10.00 – 20.00 (c).

Magazine Ad, Pard Dog Food, 10½" x 13", circa 1941, $5.00 – 10.00 (c).

Magazine Ad, Berkshire Stock-
ings, 6" x 13½", Artist: Albert
Fisher, circa 1940, $5.00 – 10.00
(c).

Magazine Ad, Camel Cigarettes, 10½" x 13", circa
1940s, $5.00 – 10.00 (c).

Magazine Ad, sewing patterns, 10" x 13¾", *Pictorial
Review*, circa January, 1952, $8.00 – 12.00 (p).

Magazine Fashion Illustration, 10" x 13¾", circa
1938, $8.00 – 12.00 (p).

Magazine Ad, Chevrolet, 10" x 13¾", Scottie: Duncan Dhu of Ardmore, *Esquire*, circa June 1936, $8.00 – 12.00 (p).

Magazine Ad, Jello, 10" x 13¾", Artist: Lyman Anderson, circa 1952, $6.00 – 8.00 (p).

Magazine Ad, Kotex, (Scotties really were used for everything!), 10" x 13¾", Artist: Tom Hall, circa 1948, $5.00 – 10.00 (p).

Magazine Ad, Carnation Milk, 10" x 13¾", circa 1945, $7.00 – 10.00 (p).

Magazine Ad, Texaco, 10" x 13¾", *Saturday Evening Post*, Artist: Morgan Dennis, November 7, 1931, $10.00 – 15.00 (p).

Magazine Ad, Gaines Meal, 10" x 13¾", *Saturday Evening Post*, September 5, 1953, $7.00 – 10.00 (p).

Magazine Ad, Gaines Meal, 10" x 13¾", circa 1945, $7.00 – 10.00 (p).

Magazine Ad, Borden's, 10" x 13¾", circa 1931, $8.00 – 12.00 (p).

Magazine Ad, General Tire and Rubber Co., 10" x 13¾", *Saturday Evening Post*, April 12, 1947, $10.00 – 15.00 (p).

Magazine Ad, Parke, Davis & Co., 10" x 13¾", circa 1957, $6.00 – 10.00 (p).

Sign, Champion Spark Plugs, metal, adapted from a 1950 magazine advertisement, circa 1990s, $15.00 – 20.00 (c).

Fruit Crate Label, Scotty's Best Washington State Pears, 10½" x 7¼", circa 1940s, $20.00 – 35.00 (p).

Magazine Ad, Polo, Ralph Lauren, 10" x 13", circa 1980s, $12.00 – 15.00 (p).

Video Movie Display, Walt Disney's *Lady and the Tramp*, paper, circa 1990s, $60.00 – 90.00 (k).

Advertisement, Spratt's Famous Dog Foods, 12" x 18", $150.00 – 180.00 (k).

Advertisement, Alka-Seltzer, 24" x 36", board, circa 1930s, $200.00 – 250.00 (k).

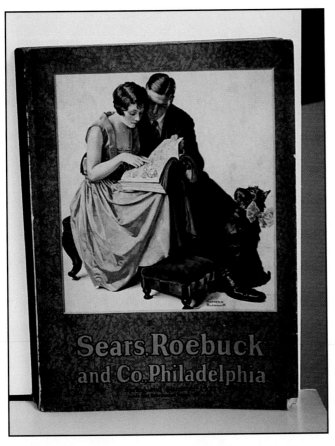

Catalog, Sears, Roebuck and Co. Philadelphia, Artist: Norman Rockwell, circa 1922, $120.00 – 150.00 (k).

Milk Bottle, glass, O. H. Hoffmire & Son Dairy, Trumansburg, New York, $75.00 – 125.00 (c).

Soda Bottles, Clown Beverages, McLaughlin, Rock Island, Illinois, circa 1930 – 1950s, $50.00 – 80.00 each (p).

Product Tin, 3" x 3¼", tin, Scotty Mild Little Cigars, Barry Cigar Factory, Quebec, Canada, circa 1910 – 1940s, $50.00 – 75.00 (k).

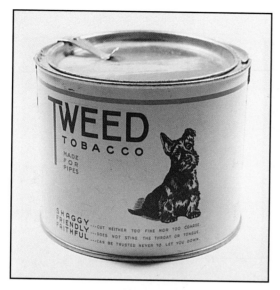

Tobacco Tin, 4" x 5", Tweed, US Tobacco Co., Richmond, Virginia, $60.00 – 90.00 (k).

Paper House, 8" x 10" x 10", Charms, $40.00 – 65.00 (k).

Fan, 10", dairy giveaway, $50.00 – 75.00 (c).

Star-Brite Oil & Grease Absorbent, circa 1973, $15.00 – 20.00 (k).

Coffee, Thomas Premium Blend, current, $6.00 – 10.00 (c).

Tea and Jam, Chesterfields Fine Foods, current, $10.00 – 25.00 each (c).

Greeting Cards and Paper Products

Vintage and current cards and paper products feature the charming Scottie. Classic or comic, he has been a common member of this category for decades.

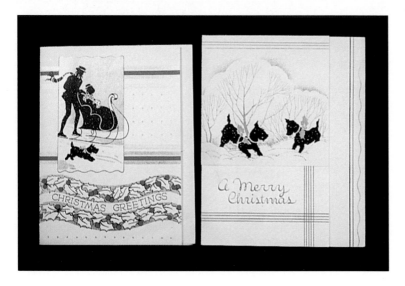

Examples of vintage Christmas cards featuring Scotties, circa 1920 – 1950s, $5.00 – 10.00 each.

Examples of vintage Christmas cards featuring Scotties, circa 1920 – 1950s, $5.00 – 10.00 each.

Examples of cards offered by Marion Needham Krupp, circa 1990s, $1.25 – 2.00 each.

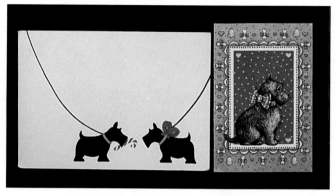

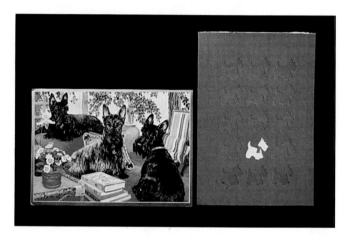

Examples of recent Christmas cards, circa 1980 – 1990s, $1.00 – 3.00 each.

Examples of vintage occasion cards, circa 1920 – 1950s, $5.00 – 10.00 each.

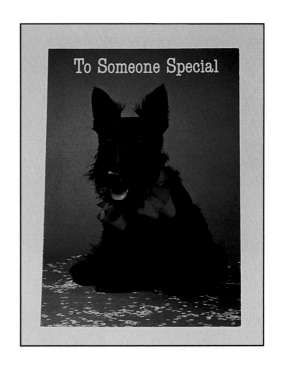

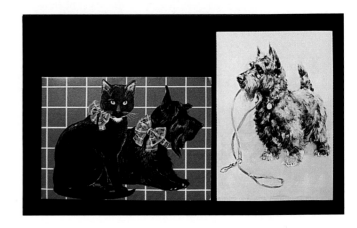

Examples of recent occasion cards, circa 1980 – 1990s, $1.00 – 3.00 each.

Examples of vintage and recent postcards, circa 1920 – 1990s, $1.00 – 7.00 each.

Card, burned paper, circa 1930s, $15.00 (c).

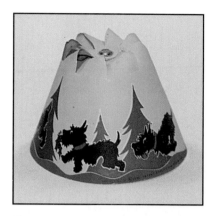

Christmas Tree Light Turbin, 2½" x 2", paper, Sail ME Co., Chicago, Whirl Glo, circa 1936, $25.00 – 40.00 (k).

Note Holder, 4½" x 6" x 1½", made in China, Artist: Mary Engelbreit, circa 1990s, $10.00 – 12.00 (p).

Box, 12" x 11" x 3", cardboard, Zonex, circa 1990, $25.00 – 35.00 (k).

Gift Bag, paper, Artist: S. Buck Baldwin, circa 1996, $2.00 – 5.00 (c).

Borders, paper, Terrific Trimmers, Trent Enterprises, Inc., circa 1981, $10.00 – 20.00 (c).

Books

As main characters, supporting actors, or cover models, Scotties have graced the pages of hundreds of books throughout the twentieth century. In the back of this book (p. 154) we have also provided a list of more books that feature the likeness of this furry fellow.

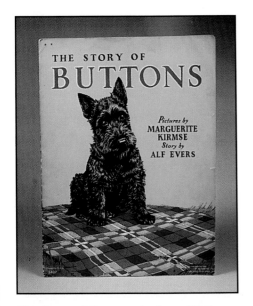

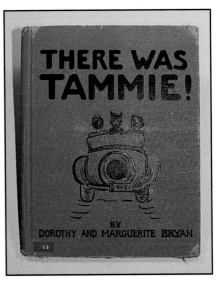

The Story of Buttons, Author: Alf Evers, Illustrator: Marguerite Kirmse, paper, circa 1936, $50.00 – 75.00 (c).

The Great Adventures of Jack, Jock and Funny, Author: Eleanor Youmans, Illustrator: Will Eannells, circa 1938, $25.00 – 50.00 (c).

There Was Tammie!, Authors and Illustrators: Dorothy and Marguerite Bryan, circa 1935, $20.00 – 40.00 (c).

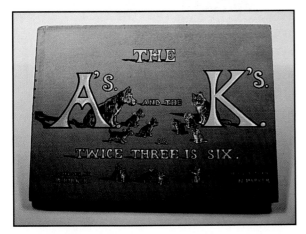

Lustige Freunde, German, $10.00 – 25.00 (c).

The A's and the K's or Twice Three Is Six, Author and Illustrator: N. Parker, Great Britain, M'Lagan & Cumming, Chromolithographers, Edinburg, circa 1910, $500.00 – 650.00 (k).

Dogs as I See Them, Author and Illustrator: Lucy Dawson (Mac), circa 1937, $40.00 – 80.00 (c).

Davy and His Dog, Illustrator: Fiore Mastri, circa 1947, $20.00 – 40.00 (c).

Dogs, Author and Illustrator: Morgan Dennis, circa 1930, $40.00 – 60.00 (c).

The Blue Book of Dogs, Author: John M. Holtzman, circa 1938, $10.00 – 20.00 (c).

I Can Read About Dogs and Puppies, Author: J. I. Anderson, Illustrator: Judith Fringuello, circa 1973, $5.00 – 10.00 (c).

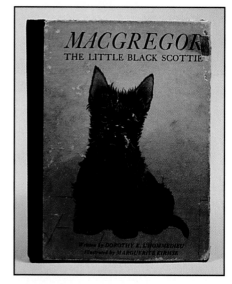

Macgregor, The Little Black Scottie, Author: Dorothy K. L'Hommedieu, Illustrator: Marguerite Kirmse, circa 1941, $75.00 – 125.00 (c).

Gallant and Dopey, Author: Marjorie Turner, $120.00 – 150.00 (k).

Angus and the Cat, Author and Illustrator: Marjorie Flack, circa 1931, $40.00 – 60.00 (c).

Angus and the Ducks, Author and Illustrator: Marjorie Flack, circa 1930, $40.00 – 60.00 (c).

Angus Lost, Author and Illustrator: Marjorie Flack, circa 1932, $40.00 – 60.00 (c).

Wag-Tail-Bess, Author and Illustrator: Marjorie Flack, circa 1933, $40.00 – 60.00 (c).

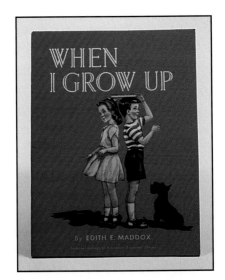

When I Grow Up, Author: Edith E. Maddox, circa 1943, $10.00 – 25.00 (c).

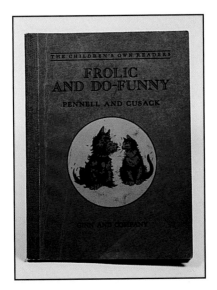

Frolic and Do-Funny, Authors: Pennell and Cusack, Illustrator: Marguerite Davis, circa 1932, $25.00 – 50.00 (c).

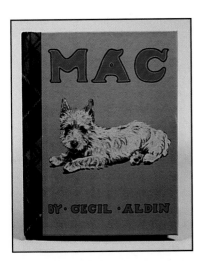

Mac, Author and Illustrator: Cecil Aldin, reprint 1997, $10.00 – 20.00 (c).

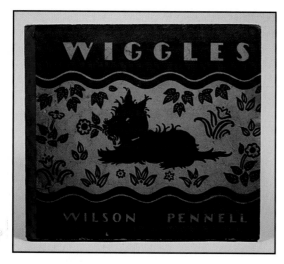

Wiggles, Authors: Wilson and Pennell, Illustrator: Marguerite Davis, circa 1936, $15.00 – 25.00 (c).

Pets, A sit in Panorama, Author and Illustrator: Theresa Kalab, circa 1944, $5.00 – 15.00 (c).

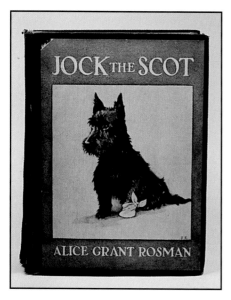

Jock the Scot, Author: Alice Grant Rosman, Illustrator: Joan Eslry, circa 1930, $75.00 – 125.00 (c).

Portrait of a Dog, Author: Mazo de la Roche, Illustrator: Morgan Dennis, circa 1930, $40.00 – 75.00 (c).

Over the Sea to Skye, Author: Robert Hutchinson, Illustrator: Rob Brown, circa 1997, $15.00 – 20.00 (c).

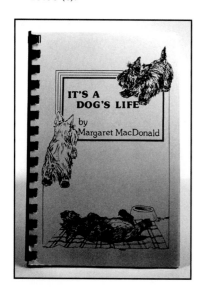

It's A Dog's Life, Author: Margaret J. MacDonald, Illustrator: Teresa Moose, circa 1994, $10.00 – 20.00 (c).

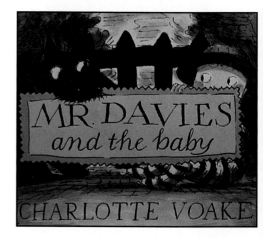

Mr. Davies and the Baby, Author and Illustrator: Charlotte Voake, circa 1996, $15.00 – 20.00 (c).

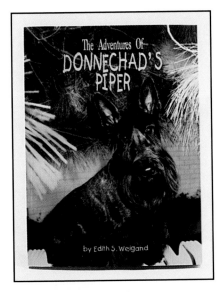

The Adventures of Donnechad's Piper,
Author: Edith S. Weigand, Illustrator:
C. A. Cleaveland, circa 1995, $12.00 –
20.00 (c).

Little Goalie, Author: Heather Lowen-
berg, Illustrator: Marilyn Mets, circa
1997, $4.00 – 8.00 (c.), and Candee
Davis's grandson, Nicholas. This is
the first Scottie collectible he found
on his own.

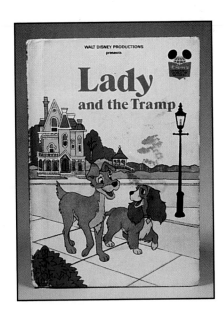

Various editions of *Lady and the Tramp* from
Walt Disney, $5.00 – 20.00 each (c).

Fine Art

Framed on your walls, in a scrapbook, or in a china cabinet, the Scottie has been a beloved subject fc numerous artists, past and present.

Wood Engraving, *Watchful Waiting*, Artist: Leo Meissner, circa 1937, $175.00 – 225.00 (c).

Wood Engraving, *It's a Small World*, Artist: Leo Meissner, circa 1930, $375.00 – 400.00 (k).

Wood Engraving, *It has Been a Busy Day*, Artist: Leo Meissner, $200.00 – 250.00 (c).

Wood Engraving, *Highland Lass*, Artist: Leo Meissner, circa 1953, $150.00 – 200.00 (c).

Wood Engraving, *Kelpie*, Artist: Leo Meissner, circa 1937, $150.00 – 200.00 (c).

Etching, *I See Myself*, Artist: Marguerite Kirmse, circa 1933, $400.00 – 425.00 (k).

Christmas Card Etching, Artist: Marguerite Kirmse, circa 1920s, $300.00 – 325.00 (k).

Etching, *Black and White*, Artist: Marguerite Kirmse, circa 1935, $450.00 – 495.00 (k).

Etching, *The Bone of Contention*, Artist: Marguerite Kirmse, circa 1938, $400.00 – 450.00 (k).

Christmas Card Etching, Artist: Marguerite Kirmse, circa 1920s, $300.00 – 325.00 (k).

Etching, *At Odds*, Artist: Marguerite Kirmse, circa 1922, $400.00 – 450.00 (k).

Etching, *The Big Splash*, Artist: Marguerite Kirmse, circa 1947, $450.00 – 500.00 (k).

Etching, *Sea Urchins*, Artist: Marguerite Kirmse, circa 1926, $475.00 – 500.00 (k).

Etching, *Anybody Home?* Artist: Marguerite Kirmse, circa 1936, $450.00 – 500.00 (k).

Etching, *The Brushwork Boy*, first etching done with a Victrola needle, Artist: Marguerite Kirmse, circa 1922, $400.00 – 425.00 (k).

Etching, *What's New?* Artist: Marguerite Kirmse, $475.00 – 500.00 (k).

Etching, *Train Time*, Artist: Marguerite Kirmse, circa 1927, $475.00 – 500.00 (k).

Etching, *We*, Artist: Marguerite Kirmse, circa 1928, $475.00 – 500.00 (k).

Etching, *Hoot Mon*, Artist: Marguerite Kirmse, circa 1929, $450.00 – 500.00 (k).

Etching, *Social Security*, Artist: Marguerite Kirmse, circa 1937, $450.00 – 500.00 (k).

Etching, Artist: Morgan Dennis, circa 1940s, $325.00 – 375.00 (c).

Etching, *The Clansmen*, Artist: Marguerite Kirmse, circa 1931, $450.00 – 500.00 (k).

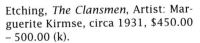

Etching, *The Campbells Are Coming*, Artist: Morgan Dennis, circa 1930s, $375.00 – 450.00 (k).

Pen and Ink, *Between the Devil & the Deep Blue Sea*, Artist: Morgan Dennis, $750.00 – 900.00 (k).

Etching, *Looking Out*, Artist: Marion Needham Krupp, circa 1990s, $40.00 – 60.00 (c).

Print, *Me and Dad*, Artist: Marion Needham Krupp, circa 1996, $10.00 – 20.00 (c).

Watercolor, untitled, executed on paper, Artist: Mabel Gear, circa 1950s, $1,000.00 – 1,200.00 (k).

Etching, *Couch Scottie*, Artist: Marion Needham Krupp, circa 1993, $60.00 – 80.00 (c). This etching is part of the AKC Museum of the Dog, St. Louis, Missouri.

Etching, *Wind-Up Scottie*, Artist: Marion Needham Krupp, circa 1998, $40.00 – 60.00 (c).

Watercolor, *A Young Scot*, executed on paper, Artist: Mabel Gear, circa 1950s, $1,000.00 – 1,200.00 (k).

Watercolor, *Where's the Food Controller*, executed on paper, Artist: Mabel Gear, circa 1950s, $1,000.00 – 1,200.00 (k).

Watercolor, *To Greet You This Christmas*, executed on board, Artist: Mabel Gear, circa 1950s, $1,000.00 – 1,200.00 (k).

Oil Painting, executed on silk, Artist: La Foret, $350.00 – 400.00 (k).

Oil Painting, executed on board, Artist: Vinton Breese, circa 1930, $1,200.00 – 1,500.00 (k).

Oil Painting, executed on board, Artist: Frank Lawson, unsigned, circa 1950s, $600.00 – 800.00 (k).

Watercolor, *Scotties*, executed on paper, Artist: Rueben Ward Binks, circa 1924, $1,500.00 – 1,800.00 (k).

Oil Painting, executed on board, Artist: Frank Lawson, circa 1950s, $750.00 – 900.00 (k).

Graphite and Wash on board, *Jock*, Artist: Will Rannells, circa 1938, $750.00 – 900.00 (k).

Print (Linoleum cut), *It's a Dog's Life*, signed, Artist: Martha Paulos, circa 1990, $150.00 – 180.00 (k).

Print, Artist: S. Thart, circa 1932, $25.00 – 50.00 (c).

Print, *Sandy and Jock*, Artist: Meta Pluckebaum, circa 1930, $40.00 – 60.00 (c).

Print, *Happy Days Are Here Again*, 15" x 19½", marked 2762 B.D., circa 1933, $25.00 – 50.00 (c).

Collage, 6½" x 6½", paper/paint/metallic stickers/confetti/cardboard, Artist: Anne Morris, Moline, Illinois, circa 1990s, $35.00 (p).

Print, *Bird's Eye View*, 11½" x 16", Artist: Gil Elvgren, circa 1938, $20.00 – 25.00 (c).

Print, Artist: Betty Boydell, circa 1937, $15.00 – 30.00 (c).

Print, *Joan and Minnie*, Artist: Lucy Dawson, circa 1930s, $20.00 – 30.00 (c).

Print, *Perfect Harmony*, reprint of etching from 1932, Artist: Louis Icart, circa 1970s, $50.00 – 75.00 (original etching could fetch $10,000.00+ at auction) (p).

Print, *Friends*, Artist: J. Knowles Hare, $10.00 – 20.00 (c).

Print, "What kind of a girl do you think I am?" $10.00 – 20.00 (c).

Plaque, "Triplets," Artist: Frozay, $10.00 – 20.00 (c).

Print, *The Loyal Scot*, Artist: Mabel Gear, circa 1990s, $40.00 – 50.00 (c).

Print, *Sons O' The Heather*, Artist: Gear, reprint circa 1990s, $10.00 – 20.00 (c).

Print, *The Scottish Terrier*, 8" x 6", Artist: Diana Thorne, circa 1945, $10.00 – 15.00 (p).

Print, *Lady and the Tramp*, premium with video purchase, circa 1998, $10.00 – 20.00 (c).

Print, "The Emmett Kelly Jr. Collection," circa 1997, $10.00 – 20.00 (c).

Collector Plate, "A Couple's Commitment," Artist: Norman Rockwell, circa 1985, $25.00 – 50.00 (c).

Plate, 10¼", porcelain, Royal Doulton, circa 1915 – 1925, $175.00 – 225.00 (k).

Plate, "A Full House," 10¼", porcelain, Wedgwood, Artist: Marguerite Kirmse, circa 1933, $300.00 – 375.00 (k).

Tray, 7½" x 5½", hammered copper, marked "Craftsman Studios," Handmade at Laguna Beach, California, #904, circa 1894 – 1923, $350.00 – 400.00 (p).

Three Dimensional Collector Plate, "A Family At Last," *Lady and the Tramp*, Disney, circa 1995, limited edition of 7,500, $75.00 – 100.00 (c).

Plate, 6" x 6", copper, Artist: Francisco Rebaj, New York, New York, circa late 1930 – 1950s, $150.00 – 175.00 (p).

Silhouette, 4" x 5", reverse painting on convex glass, Benton Glass Co., circa 1940s, $40.00 – 55.00 (p).

Silhouette, 4" x 5", reverse painting on convex glass, Benton Glass Co., circa 1940s, $40.00 – 55.00 (p).

Silhouette, 4" x 5", reverse painting on convex glass, Benton Glass Co., circa 1940s, $40.00 – 55.00 (p).

Silhouette, 4" x 5", reverse painting on convex glass, Benton Glass Co., circa 1940s, $40.00 – 55.00 (p).

Toys and Games

Furry or flat, soft or hard, on wheels or stationary, Scotties make wonderful playthings.

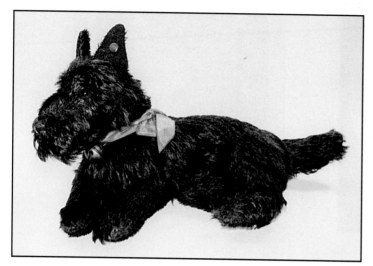

Stuffed, 11" x 6" x 6", mohair, Steiff button in ear, $400.00 – 450.00 (k).

Stuffed, 15" x 5" x 9", mohair, Steiff #1325,02, circa 1940s, $400.00 – 450.00 (k).

Stuffed, 10" x 4" x 8", mohair, Shuco, $180.00 – 225.00 (k).

Stuffed, 15" x 5" x 12", mohair, Steiff Scotty #1328,02, $450.00 – 500.00 (k).

Stuffed, 9" x 5" x 8", mohair, Steiff, $300.00 – 350.00 (k).

Stuffed, 7" x 2½" x 6", mohair/glass eyes, $275.00 – 325.00 (k).

Stuffed, 18" x 17" x 16", mohair/metal/wood, $180.00 – 200.00 (k).

Stuffed, 9½" x 5" x 8", mohair/metal/wood, $150.00 – 180.00 (k).

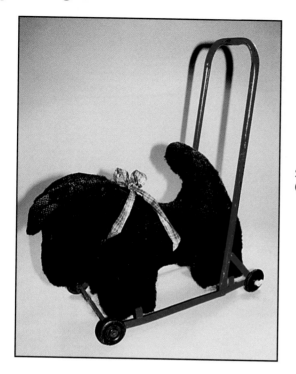

Stuffed, 15" x 6" x 10", mohair/metal/wood, $200.00 – 225.00 (k).

Stuffed, 10" x 5½" x 11", mohair/metal/wood, $120.00 – 150.00 (k).

Stuffed, 3" x 4" x 1", wood/silk fur/glass eyes, Germany, circa early 1900s, $55.00 – 65.00 (p).

Stuffed, 6" x 3" x 5", mohair, circa 1940s, $20.00 – 50.00 (c).

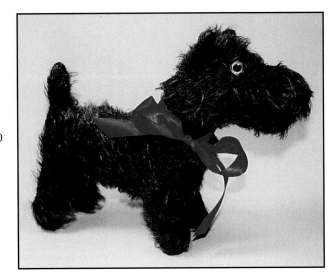

Stuffed, 9" x 4" x 7", mohair, circa 1950s, $25.00 – 60.00 (c).

Stuffed, 6" x 2" x 6", plush, circa 1940s, $15.00 – 25.00 (c).

Stuffed, 9" x 4½" x 8", mohair, circa 1940s, $50.00 – 75.00 (c).

Stuffed, 8" x 4" x 7", plush, circa 1950s, $15.00 – 40.00 (c).

Stuffed, 14" x 7" x 9", bear fur, circa 1950s, $75.00 – 100.00 (c).

Stuffed, 5" x 2" x 4", mohair, moving mouth, $80.00 – 110.00 (k).

Stuffed, 8" x 3" x 7", mohair, walks when leash is pulled, $120.00 – 150.00 (k).

Stuffed, 12" x 6" x 12", plush, Steiff Blacky terrier #4184/35, circa 1980 – 1990s, $125.00 – 175.00 (c).

Stuffed, 6" x 4" x 8", plush, Jock beanie, Disney, circa 1998, $6.00 – 10.00 (c).

Stuffed, 12" x 8" x 12", plush, The Heritage Collection, Ganz, circa 1990s, $25.00 – 35.00 (c).

Stuffed, 8" x 2" x 8", plush, Great Scots, North American Bear Co., circa 1990s, $10.00 – 15.00 (c).

Stuffed, 5" x 3" x 5", plush, barks, Dakin, circa 1990s, $5.00 – 10.00 (c).

Stuffed, 16" x 8" x 10", plush, circa 1997, $10.00 – 20.00 (c).

Stuffed, 13" x 6" x 10", plush, barks/wags tail, circa 1990s, $20.00 – 30.00 (c).

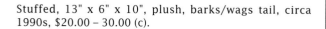

Stuffed, 4½" x 4½" x 13", plush, Nice Stuff, circa 1990s, $10.00 – 20.00 (c).

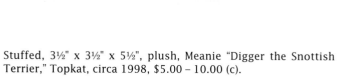

Stuffed, 3½" x 3½" x 5½", plush, Meanie "Digger the Snottish Terrier," Topkat, circa 1998, $5.00 – 10.00 (c).

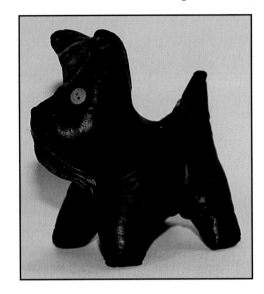

Stuffed, 5½" x 5½", vinyl/velvet, circa 1950s, $12.00 – 20.00 (p).

Doll, 8", Jean's Dolls, Wendy Walks Her Dog, Madame Alexander, circa 1980s, $100.00 – 150.00 (c).

Shirley Temple Doll, vinyl, original dress, felt, opening/closing eyes, Ideal, circa 1950s, $175.00 – 225.00 (k).

Doll, Kelly, 4½", Mattel, Scottie hairbrush, circa 1998, $5.00 – 10.00 (c).

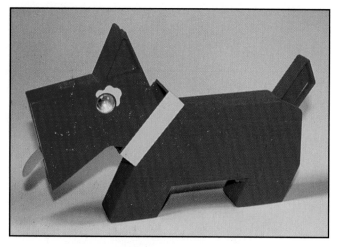

Flashlight, 7" x 1" x 5", plastic, Ray-O-Vac, circa 1950s, $25.00 – 50.00 (c).

Cereal Premium, 1¾", plastic, marked "Walt Disney Prod. Inc.," circa 1950s, $10.00 – 15.00 (c).

Picture Record, 33⅓" RPM, Disney's *Lady and the Tramp*, $30.00 – 60.00 (k).

Baby Rattle, 8" long, Klak-ker, made in USA, $120.00 – 150.00 (k).

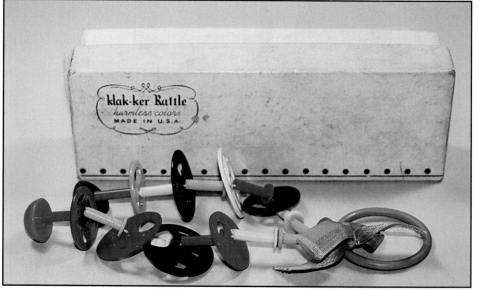

Wind-up Toy, 5" x 2" x 4", wool/metal, Shuco, made in US Zone, Germany, circa 1940 – 1950s, $200.00 – 250.00 (k).

Wind-up Toy, 5" x 2" x 3½", wool/metal, $80.00 – 110.00 (k).

Wind-up Toy, 3½" x 3½" x 1", wood/wool/plastic eyes/metal key, Japan, shakes sock/wags tail, circa 1930s, $65.00 – 80.00 (p).

Wind-up Toy, 8" x 2" x 3½", $80.00 – 120.00 (k).

Wind-up Toy, 8" x 2" x 3½", celluloid Scottie/metal shoe, $80.00 – 125.00 (k).

Toys, 5" x 2" x 4", tin, Wee Scottie, Marx Toys, $200.00 – 250.00, with wooden front legs; without wooden front legs, $125.00 – 150.00 (k).

Push-button Toy, 4", accoutrements, circa 1997, $5.00 – 10.00 (c).

Squeak Toy, 3½" x 4½" x 8½", rubber, circa 1940s, $100.00 – 120.00 (k).

Squeak Toy, 2" x 3" x 4", Jock, part of set, *Lady and the Tramp*, Disney, circa 1998, $15.00 – 25.00 (c) (full set includes Lady, Tramp, Trusty, and Si or Am the Cat).

Squeak Toy, 2" x 4" x 4½", latex, Lanco, Vo-Toys, Inc., Spain, circa 1990s, $5.00 – 10.00 (c).

Puppet, 9" x 13", mohair, $150.00 – 180.00 (k).

Puppet, 9" x 3", mohair/wool/cotton, $100.00 – 120.00 (k).

Puppet, 7" x 5" x 6", rubber/cloth, $40.00 – 60.00 (k).

Puppet Head, 3½", rubber, Toto from *The Wizard of Oz*, circa 1960s, $20.00 – 40.00 (p). Note: One of eight puppets was attached to selected Procter & Gamble products and by sending a proof of purchase and 25¢ to the manufacturer, a theater for the puppets could be obtained.

Ball, 2½", rubber, $25.00 – 30.00 (k).

Toy, 3½" x 1" x 2¼", rubber, circa 1950s, $5.00 – 10.00 (c).

Toy, 3½" x 1" x 2¼", rubber, circa 1950s, $5.00 – 10.00 (c).

Music Maker, 3" x 5", tin, $60.00 – 80.00 (k).

Top, 7" x 8", tin, Chad Valley Co., Ltd., Harborne, England, Toymakers to her Majesty the Queen, $110.00 – 125.00 (k).

Car, 3½" x 1½" x 1½", metal, Spratts Bonio Ovals & Dog Cakes, Days-Gone, England, Lledo, circa 1990, $40.00 – 50.00 (k).

Paint Set, 5" x 10", England, circa 1960s, $15.00 – 20.00 (c).

Shoofly (and Nicholas), 30" x 12½" x 15", wood, circa 1930s, $150.00 – 175.00 (c).

Seat decoration of Shoofly shown above.

Toy, 11" x 3" x 8", wood/jointed, Germany, $150.00 – 180.00 (k).

Pull Toys, large 2½" x 5" x 4¼", small 2¾" x 1¾" x 2½", composition wood/wood, Hubley, "made of the new material: Huboid," circa 1940s, $25.00 – 100.00 each (k).

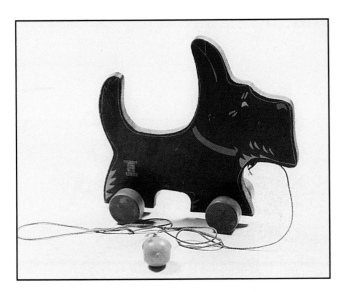

Pull Toy, 6" x 2" x 5", wood, Fisher Price, circa 1950, $50.00 – 60.00 (k).

Pull Toy, 3¼" x 2" x 3½", wood/rubber wheels, $40.00 – 60.00 (k).

Candy Container, 6" x 4" x 8", papier maché, England, $60.00 – 80.00 (k).

Puzzle, "His First Christmas," paper, $60.00 – 80.00 (k).

Puzzle, 10" x 12", paper, Educational Playthings, Inc., circa 1939, $80.00 – 120.00 (k).

Puzzle, 8" x 10", paper, circa 1950s, $10.00 – 20.00 (c).

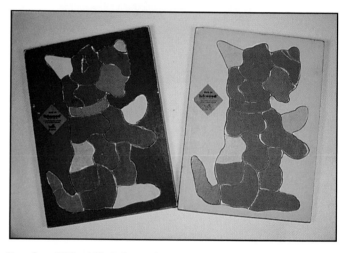

Puzzles, 8¾" x 12", Tekwood, circa 1950s, $15.00 – 25.00 each (c).

Scottish Terrier Chip, 1¼", plastic/paper, given out with Humpty Dumpty Potato Chips, part of a set of 60 dogs, Canada, circa 1940s, $3.00 – 5.00 (p).

Teeter Totter, 16" x 18" x 6", wood/iron, marked "R & R Manufacturers, Aledo, Ill, T-Totter," (Patty Baugh was born in Aledo), circa 1940s, cannot be priced as it is the only one we have heard of or seen (p).

Kaleidoscope, 9", circa 1990s, $8.00 – 12.00 (c).

Card Holder, 6" x 3½" x 3½", metal, Bradley & Hubbard, circa 1920s, $80.00 – 100.00 (k).

Playing Cards, circa 1930s, $10.00 – 30.00 per deck (p).

Playing Cards, circa 1930s, $10.00 – 30.00 per deck (p).

Playing Cards, United States Playing Card Company, circa 1932, $10.00 – 30.00 per deck (p).

Playing Cards, left, gift from Wee Scott's 1997 convention, circa 1990s, $1.00 per card; right, made in England, advertisement for Valstar Weatherwear and Travel Wear, circa 1930s, $10.00 – 30.00 per deck (p).

Playing Cards, circa 1930s, $10.00 – 30.00 per deck (p).

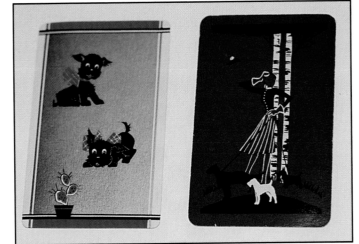

Playing Cards, circa 1930s, $10.00 – 30.00 per deck (p).

Playing Cards, left, marked "C982-62P3032," circa 1930s, $10.00 – $30.00 per deck; right, Fifth Avenue Playing Cards, circa 1930s, $25.00 – 30.00 per deck (p).

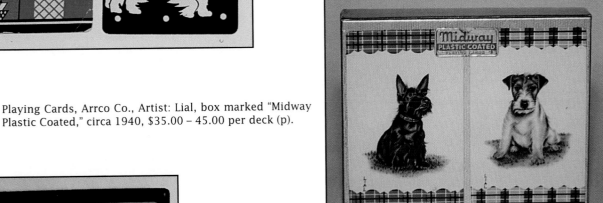

Playing Cards, Arrco Co., Artist: Lial, box marked "Midway Plastic Coated," circa 1940, $35.00 – 45.00 per deck (p).

Playing Cards, marked "Buddies, A Western Product, H 7694-25R, made in USA," Artist: Lucy Dawson, circa 1930s, $25.00 – 35.00 per deck (p).

Spirits and Libations

Celebrate with the "Scotch" Terrier of Black & White fame.

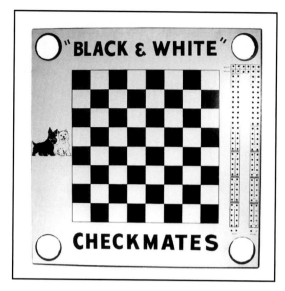

Game Board, 24" x 24", wood, $120.00 – 150.00 (k).

Bottle Display, Black & White Scotch, papier maché, holds one bottle behind dogs, circa 1950s, $50.00 – 60.00 (p).

Black & White Scotch Bottles, glass bottles/paper label, J. Buchannan & Co. Ltd., England, circa 1955 – 1988, $5.00 – 12.00 each (p).

Tumblers, 4", glass, circa 1960s, $10.00 – 15.00 each (c).

Party Favor, 2½" x 1" x 2", marked "Scotch and Soda," wood/plastic/chenille stems/wool, circa 1940s, $5.00 – 8.00 (p).

Flask, 1½" x 4" x 6", plastic/metal, circa 1950s, $12.00 – 15.00 (p).

Advertisement, 18" x 28", two-sided board, circa 1972, $60.00 – 80.00 (k).

Magazine Advertisement, Black & White Scotch, Artist: Morgan Dennis, $10.00 – 25.00 (k).

Magazine Advertisement, 10" x 13", Black & White Scotch, Artist: Morgan Dennis, circa 1956, $6.00 – 10.00 (p).

Magazine Advertisement, Holiday, 10" x 13", Black & White Scotch, Artist: Morgan Dennis, circa January 1950, $15.00 – 20.00 (p).

Magazine Advertisement, 10" x 1" x 3", Black & White Scotch, circa 1971, $9.00 – 12.00 (p).

Magazine Advertisement, 10" x 13", Black & White Scotch, circa 1963, $6.00 – 10.00 (p).

Magazine Advertisement, 10" x 13", Black & White Scotch, Artist: Morgan Dennis, circa 1951, $6.00 – 10.00 (p).

Magazine Advertisement, 5" x 13", Black & White Scotch, Artist: Morgan Dennis, circa 1953, $3.00 – 5.00 (p).

Magazine Advertisement, 5" x 13", Black & White Scotch, Artist: Morgan Dennis, circa 1954, $3.00 – 5.00 (p).

Magazine Advertisement, 5" x 13", Black & White Scotch, Artist: Morgan Dennis, circa 1953, $3.00 – 5.00 (p).

Magazine Advertisement, 5" x 13", Black & White Scotch, Artist: Morgan Dennis, circa 1947, $3.00 – $5.00 (p).

Magazine Advertisement, 5" x 13", Black & White Scotch, Artist: Morgan Dennis, circa 1959, $3.00 – 5.00 (p).

Magazine Advertisement, 5" x 13", Black & White Scotch, Artist: Morgan Dennis, circa 1958, $3.00 – 5.00 (p).

Magazine Advertisement, 5" x 13", Black & White Scotch, Artist: Morgan Dennis, circa 1958, $3.00 – 5.00 (p).

Magazine Advertisement, 5" x 13", Black & White Scotch, Artist: Morgan Dennis, circa 1945, $3.00 – 5.00 (p).

Magazine Advertisement, 5" x 13", Black & White Scotch, Artist: Morgan Dennis, circa 1953, $3.00 – 5.00 (p).

Magazine Advertisement, 5" x 13", Black & White Scotch, Artist: Morgan Dennis, circa 1957, $3.00 – 5.00 (p).

Scottie Sightings

In the Movies

Though rarely the star, the Scottish terrier and Scottie collectibles appear in motion pictures. Here are a few in which we have spotted our favorite fellow:

Angus Lost — a starring role
Another Thin Man — he's definitely a rogue in this one
Buffy the Vampire Slayer — Scottie sweater
Disney Christmas — cartoon
Eleanor and Franklin — a Fala look-alike
Father Goose — Black & White Scotch fans take note
Forsaking All Others — just a bit part
Groundhog Day — watch the windowsill near the beginning
Kennel Murder Case, The — they're everywhere
Lady and the Tramp — best supporting actor award here
Light that Failed, The — drama for sure
McHale's Navy Joins the Air Force — cameo as Fala
Men in Black — fireplace scene
Remains of the Day — butler's bedroom wall
Sleeper — a robot Scottie
Stand-In, The — Bogart's companion
Step Mom — Scottie pajamas
Under the Rainbow — near the end
You've Got Mail — bookstore scene

In Books and Old Readers

Books

This list includes titles, authors, and illustrators of just a small sampling of books with Scottie Dogs as the main character, supporting character, or cover model.

Title	Author	Illustrator
ABC Dogs	Tice, Clara	Tice, Clara
About Friends	Tudyman, Al	McFarland, Thomas L.
Adventures of Donnechad's Piper, The	Weigand, Edith S.	Cleaveland, C. A.
Affectionately, F.D.R.	Roosevelt, James and Sidney Shalett	photographs
All About Pets	Bianco, Margery Williams	Gilkison, Grace
Angus and the Cat	Flack, Marjorie	Flack, Marjorie
Angus and the Ducks	Flack, Marjorie	Flack, Marjorie
Angus Lost	Flack, Marjorie	Flack, Marjorie
Animals (cloth)		
Around the World with Children and Dogs	Thorne, Diana	Thorne, Diana
Best Dog Stories	Various	Various
Best in Children's Books/Angus and the Cat	Flack, Marjorie	Flack, Marjorie
Best in Children's Books/Angus and the Ducks	Flack, Marjorie	Flack, Marjorie
Big Book of Dogs, The	Sutton, Felix	Leason, Percy
Black Dog Mystery, The	Queen, Ellery Jr.	Sanderson, William
Black Rod	Poultney, C. B.	Poultney, C. B.
Blue Book of Dogs, The	Holzworth, John	
Bonnie Bits O' Bonnie Scotland	Junior, Allan	photographs
Book of the Scottish Terrier 1948	Ewing, Fayette	photographs
Child's Book of Dogs, A	Henderson, Luis M	Henderson, Luis M.
Child's Garden of Verses, A	Stevenson, Robert Louis	Trimmer, George
Chipper	Whitman Publishers	
Closest Companion	Ward, Geoffrey C.	photographs
Code of the Woosters, The	Wodehouse, P. G.	
Color Nature Library, The Dog's	Wratten, Peggy	photographs
Come Away Home	Smith, Alison	Haeffele, Deborah
Come Back Puppies	Ormerod, Jan	
Come Play With Me	Watts, Mabel	

Complete Scottish Terrier 1976	Marvin, John T.	photographs
Crazy Quilt Circus Pony	Brown, Paul	Brown, Paul
Dabble Duck	Ellis, Anne Leo	Truesdell, Sue
Davy and His Dog	Mastri, Fiore	
Dog Book, The	Terhune, Albert Payson	Thorne, Diana
Dog Friends	Scott, A. O.	Scott, A. O.
Dog Stories	Held, John Jr.	Held, John Jr.
Dogs	Dennis, Morgan	Dennis, Morgan
Dogs (M. Kirmse's Dogs)	Kirmse, Marguerite	Kirmse, Marguerite
Dogs As I See Them	Dawson, Lucy	Dawson, Lucy
Dogs Rough and Smooth	Dawson, Lucy	Dawson, Lucy
Dogs, An Album of Drawings	Thorne, Diana	Thorne, Diana
Dogs, Paintings and Stories	Thorne, Diana	Thorne, Diana
Drawing Dogs	Cook, Gladys Emerson	Cook, Gladys Emerson
Eleanor: The Years Alone	Lash, Joseph P.	photographs
Eleanor Roosevelt We Remember, The	Douglas, Helen Gahagan	photographs
Eric Gurney's Pop-Up Book of Dogs	Gurney, Eric	
Eyes of Nature, Dogs	Koslow, Phillip	photographs
Fala Factor, The	Kaminsky, Stuart M.	
Fala: A President's Dog	Mussey, Virginia Howell	Van Doren, Margaret
Famous Dog Stories	Various	Stover, Wallace
Famous Dog Stories	Cooper, Page, ed.	Thorne, Diana
Famous Mascots & K-9s	Harmer, Mabel	
FDR, A Centenary Remembrance	Alsop, Joseph	photographs
FDR's Last Year	Bishop, Jim	photographs
First Book of Dogs, The	Taber, Gladys	Kuhn, Bob
Friendly Animals Picture Book	Trimmer, George	
Gallant and Dopey	Turner, Marjorie	
Glover's Dog Book 1937		
Gone to the Dogs	Conant, Susan	
Great Adventures of Jack, Jock and Funny	Youmans, Eleanor	Rannells, Will
His Apologies	Kipling, Rudyard	Aldin, Cecil
Hollywood Dogs	Suares, J. C.	
How to Raise and Train a Scottish Terrier 1960	Gannon, Robert	VanDerMeid, Louise
I Can Read About Dogs and Puppies	Anderson, J. I.	Fringuello, Judith
It's A Dog's Life	MacDonald, Margaret	Moose, Teresa
Jock and Jill	Huneker, Maida	Dennis, Morgan
Jock the Scot	Rosman, Alice Grant	Esley, Joan
Just Pups	Barker, K. F.	Barker, K. F.
Kellogg's Cookbook, 1933		
Kittens and Puppies, Horses and Rabbits and Insects, Turtles and Birds	Koehler, Cynthia Iliff and Alvin	
Lady	Armstrong, Samuel	
Lady	Hubbard, Allan and Gene Wolfe	
Lady and the Tramp	Random House Book Club Edition	
Lady and the Tramp, Golden Book	Slater, Teddy	Langley, Bill and Ron
Dias		
Little Dog Sniff and the Twins	Smith, Geraldine Foster	Henneberger, Robert
Little Goalie	Lowenberg, Heather	Mets, Marilyn
Little Golden Book of Dogs	Jones, Nita	Gergely, Tibor
Mac	Aldin, Cecil	Aldin, Cecil
Mac Goes to School	Wynkoop, Margaret L.	Richie, Robert Yarnell
Macgregor the Little Black Scottie	L'Hommedieu, Dorothy K.	Kirmse, Marguerite
Mammoth Paint Book	Rowe, Louise	Henderson, Luis
Mary Engelbreit, The Art and the Artist	Regan, Patrick with Mary Engelbreit	Engelbreit, Mary
Mister Cinders: The Tale of Shanghi Scot	Momber	
Morgan Dennis Dog Book	Dennis, Morgan	Dennis, Morgan
Mr. Davies and the Baby	Voake, Charlotte	Voake, Charlotte
Mr. M'Tavish	Bullard, Marion	Bullard, Marion
My Little Book of Dogs, Golden Tell-A-Tale Book	Draper, Delores	Stone, David K.
My Story — The Official Fala Coloring Book	Pinto, Israel	Pinto, Israel
Mythology of Dogs, The	Hausman, Gerald and Loretta	photographs
Nobody's Doll	DeLeeuw, Adele	Vaughn, Anne
Over the Sea to Skye	Hutchinson, Robert	Brown, Rob
Peggy Brown & the Big Haunted House	Heinsenfelt, Kathryn	Valleyly, Henry
Peggy Brown & the Jewel of Fire	Heinsenfelt, Kathryn	Valleyly, Henry
Peggy Brown & the Mystery Basket	Heinsenfelt, Kathryn	Valleyly, Henry
Peggy Brown & the Runaway Auto Trailer	Heinsenfelt, Kathryn	Valleyly, Henry
Peggy's Pokey and Other Stories	Malvern, Corrine	

Title	Author	
Pet for Peter	Grider, Dorothy	
Pet Scottish Terrier 1958	Snethen, Mr. and Mrs. T. H.	Dennis, Morgan
Pete	Robinson, Tom	Dennis, Morgan
Pets-a Sit in Panorama	Kalab, Theresa	Kalab, Theresa
Pets at the Whitehouse	Carmer, Carl	Savitt, Sam
Playtime Paint Book	Whitman Publishers	
Portrait of a Dog	DeLaRoche, Mazo	Dennis, Morgan
Primrose Day	Haywood, Carolyn	Haywood, Carolyn
Puppies	Thorne, Diana	Thorne, Diana
Puppies (Linenette)	Sam'l Gabriel Sons and Company	
Puppies on Parade	Helfand, Karen	Eubank, Mary Grace
Puppy Stories	Beaudry, Evien G.	Thorne, Diana
President FDR and Best Friend Fala Coloring Book	Anderson, Larry and Diana	Darling, Diana
Rand McNally Junior Elf	Stahlmann, Catherine	Wilde, Irma
Real Tales of Real Dogs	Terhune, Albert Payson	Thorne, Diana
Rubaiyat of a Scotch Terrier	Collins, Sewell	Collins, Sewell
Scalawag the Scottie	Faison, Mabel Hubbard	Foy, Ottilie
Scotch Dhu	Poultney, C. B.	Poultney, C. B.
Scottie Showcase	Newton, Donna	Krupp, Marion
Sergeant's Dog Book 1945	Dennis, Morgan	Dawson, Lucy
Story of Buttons, The	Evers, Alf	Kirmse, Marguerite
Story of Eleanor Roosevelt, The	Hickok, Lorena A.	Barss, William
There Was Tammie	Bryan, Dot and Marg	Bryan, Dot and Marg
Thy Servant a Dog	Kipling, Rudyard	Kirmse, Marguerite
Thy Servant a Dog	Kipling, Rudyard	Stampa, G. L.
Tiny Tots Object Book	Whitman Publishing Co.	
Treasury of Dog Stories, A	Various	Dennis, Wesley
Treasury of Scottie Dog Collectibles	Davis, Candace L. Sten Davis and Patricia Baugh	photographs
True Dog Stories	Terhune, Albert Payson	Thorne, Diana
True Story of Fala, The	Suckley, Margaret and Alice Dalgliesh	Fairchild, E.N.
Wag-Tail-Bess	Flack, Marjorie	Flack, Marjorie
Waggery Town	Duncan, Philip	Duncan, Philip
Wagging Tails	Henry, Marguerite	Dennis, Wesley
What Shall We Do When We Go Out? Traditional Song	Halpern, Shari	
Where are you?	See, Sam	Lieberman, Frank
Whopper Paint Book	Abigail	
Wiggles	Wilson, Clara O. and Mary E. Pennell	Davis, Marguerite
Wonder Book of Puppies, The	Koehler, Cynthia Iliff and Alvin	
Woodcuts of New York	Mueller, Hans Alexander	Mueller, Hans Alexaner
World Book of Dogs	Tatham, Julie Campbell	Megergee, Edwin

Old Readers

Title	Author	
All Around Us	Beauchamp, Crampton and Gray	
Along The Way	Hildreth, Gertrude	Berry, Erick, F. T. Chapman, Joan Esley
At Play	Hildreth, Gertrude	Waterall and Corrine Pauli
Day In and Day Out	O'Donnell, Mabel	Hoopes, Florence and Margaret and Alice Carey
Down the River Road	O'Donnell, Mabel	Hoopes, Florence and Margaret
Elson Gray Basic Reader Primer	Elson, William, William S. Gray and Lura E. Runkel Huford	Story, Miriam
Everyday Life Primer	Gehres, Ethel Maltby	photographs
Frolic and Do-Funny	Pennell, Mary E. and Alice M. Cusack	Davis, Marguerite
I Know a Secret	Hildreth, Gertrude	Waterall, Corrine Pauli and Jacob B. Abbott
Little Lost Dog	Wright, Lula	Bromhall, Winifred
Mac and Muff	Hildreth, Gertrude	Waterall, Corrine Pauli
More Streets and Roads	Gray, William S.	Arbuthnot, May Hill
Our New Friends, The New	Various	
On Four Feet	Gates, Arthur I.	Huber, Miriam Blanton and Frank S. Salisbury
Pets and Play Times	Grady, William E.	Hoopes, Florence and Margaret Freeman
Sniff	Tippett, James S. and Martha Kelly	Dennis, Morgan
Through the Gate	Various	Holland, Janice and Sally Tate
Today We Go	Gates, Arthur I.	Huber, Miriam Blanton and Frank S. Salisbury
Twins, The, Tom and Don	Hildreth, Gertrude	Waterall, Corinne Pauli
We Are Neighbors	Ousley, Odille	
When I Grow Up	Maddox, Edith E.	

Scottie Merchandisers and Publications

Angus Stitches, P.O. Box 130, Slaterville Springs, NY 14881, e-mail: fancywork@clarityconnect.com, website:www.clarityconnect.com/webpages/fancywork/Angus.htm

Biscotti's Boutique, 6 Carter Street, Hanover, NH 03755, e-mail: lorden@valley.net, website:scotties.com/lorden.html

Campbell's Scottish Terriers, 6880 Tepper Drive, Clifton, VA 20124-1638, 703-266-7522, e-mail: KidFixerC3@aol.com, website: campbellscotties.com

Colter Designs, P.O. Box 168, Berkshire, NY 13736, e-mail: TheresaT@clarityconnect.com

DB Designs, The Scottie Sampler, P.O. Box 450, Danielson, CT 06239-0450, 860-564-6660, e-mail: dbohnlein@snet.net

The Dog's House, 2511 Irving Road, Thaxton, VA 24174, 800-851-6899

FDR Library, The Museum Store, 511 Albany Post Road, Hyde Park, NY 12538, 800-FDR-VISIT

In The Company of Dogs, P.O. Box 7071, Dover, DE 19903, 800-924-5050

Marion Krupp Art, P. O. Box 408, Solebury, PA 18963, 215-862-5837, e-mail: scothund@voicenet.com, website: www.cyberscots.com/krupp

Official Fala Catalog, American Heritage Collections, Inc., 9004H Yellow Brick Road, Baltimore, MD 21237, 1-800-788-3196, website: www.americanheritage-1.com

Puttin' on the Dog, 5140 Shadow Path Lane, Lilburn, GA 30247-7703, 800-720-8005, website: www.puttinonthedog.com

RRazzy's Collection, P.O. Box 2576, Merrifield, VA 22116, 1-888-772-9997 website: www.rrazzy.com

Scottie Obsession, 1092 Welwyn Drive, Westerville, OH 43081-5517, e-mail: falapink@iwaynet.net, website: www.iwaynet.net/~falapink

Scottie Treasures, P.O. Box 130, Slaterville Springs, NY 14881, e-mail: fancywork@clarityconnect.com, website: www.clarityconnect.com/webpages/fancywork/treasures.htm

Scotty's Gifts & Accessories, 3802 Ivey Lane, Lilburn, GA 30047-2134, 800-638-2338, e-mail: Scottys@scottysgifts.com, website: www.scottysgifts.com/home.html

Tartan Terrier, 4812 S. 284th Place, Auburn, WA 98001-1908, e-mail: tartanterrier@earthlink.net

Tartan Scottie, *Great Scots Magazine*, 1028 Girard NE, Albuquerque, NM 87106, 800-766-6091, e-mail: scottie@nmia.com

Tinkers Treasures, 35609 Persimmon St., Yucaipa, CA 92399, 909-797-6982

Wilderstein, Friends of Fala, P.O. Box 383, Rhinebeck, NY 12572, 914-876-4818

Bibliography

Bohnlein, David, ed. *Celluloid Pins*, Scottie Sampler. Winchester, Virginia: DB Designs, Volume 13, Number 4, August, 1996, 5-7.

Brenner, Robert. *Christmas Past.* West Chester, Pennsylvania: Schiffer Publishing Ltd., 1985.

Dale, Jean. *The Charlton Standard Catalogue of Royal Doulton Animals, 1st ed.* Toronto, Canada: The Charlton Press, 1994.

Florence, Gene. *The Collector's Encyclopedia of Akro Agate, Revised ed.* Paducah, Kentucky: Collector Books, 1992.

———. *The Collector's Encyclopedia of Depression Glass, 12th ed.* Paducah, Kentucky: Collector Books, 1996

Garmon, Lee and Dick Spencer. *Glass Animals of the Depression Era.* Paducah, Kentucky: Collector Books, 1993.

Hahn, Frank L. and Paul Kikeli. *Collector's Guide to Heisey and Heisey by Imperial Glass Animals.* Lima, Ohio: Golden Era Publications, 1991.

Hall, Doris and Burdell. *Morton Potteries: 99 Years, Vol. 2.* Gas City, Indiana: L-W Book Sales, 1995.

Huxford, Sharon and Bob, ed. *Schroeder's Antiques Price Guide, 15th ed.* Paducah, Kentucky: Collector Books, 1998.

Kuritzky, Louis. *Collector's Guide to Bookends.* Paducah, Kentucky: Collector Books, 1998.

Luckey, Carl F. *Luckey's Hummel Figurines and Plates, 11th ed.* Iola, Wisconsin: Krause Publishing Co., 1997.

Metal Art Goods by Hubley catalog, Lancaster, Pennsylvania: Hubley Manufacturing Co., 1940 – 41.

National Cambridge Collector's Club. *Cambridge Glass, Value Guide No. CG-176,* Paducah, Kentucky: Collector Books, 1976.

National Cambridge Collector's, Inc. *Colors in Cambridge Glass.* Paducah, Kentucky: Collector Books, 1984.

Newton, Donna and Marion Needham Krupp. *Scottie Showcase.* Columbus, Indiana: Country Scottie, 1988.

Newton, Donna. "Leo Meissner, Scottie Owner--Artist," Scottie Sampler. Columbus, Indiana: Wee Scots, Inc. Volume 13, Number 1, Fall, 1995, 1-2.

Rittenhouse, Judy and Ron. *Hubley Art Goods Price Guide.* Lancaster, Pennsylvania: Hubley Manufacturing Co., 1985.

Scarfone, Jay and William Stillman. *The Wizard of Oz Collectibles Treasury.* West Chester, Pennsylvania: Schiffer Publishing Ltd., 1992.

Weatherman, Hazel Marie. *Colored Glassware of the Depression Era 2.* Ozark, Missouri: Glassbooks, 1974.

———. *The Decorated Tumbler.* Springfield, Missouri: Glassbooks, Inc., 1978.

Whitmyer, Margaret and Kenn. *Bedroom and Bathroom Glassware of the Depression Years.* Paducah, Kentucky: Collector Books, 1990.

———. *Christmas Collectibles,* Paducah, Kentucky: Collector Books, 1987.

———. *Collector's Encyclopedia of Children's Dishes,* Paducah, Kentucky: Collector Books, 1995.

COLLECTOR BOOKS
Informing Today's Collector

DOLLS, FIGURES & TEDDY BEARS

2079	**Barbie** Doll Fashion, Volume I, Eames	$24.95
3957	**Barbie** Exclusives, Rana	$18.95
4557	**Barbie**, The First 30 Years, Deutsch	$24.95
3810	**Chatty Cathy** Dolls, Lewis	$15.95
4559	Collectible **Action Figures**, 2nd Ed., Manos	$17.95
1529	Collector's Encyclopedia of **Barbie** Dolls, DeWein/Ashabraner	$19.95
2211	Collector's Encyclopedia of **Madame Alexander Dolls**, 1965-1990, Smith	$24.95
4863	Collector's Encyclopedia of **Vogue Dolls**, Stover/Izen	$29.95
4861	Collector's Guide to **Tammy**, Sabulis/Weglewski	$18.95
3967	Collector's Guide to **Trolls**, Peterson	$19.95
1799	**Effanbee** Dolls, Smith	$19.95
5253	Story of **Barbie**, 2nd Ed., Westenhouser	$24.95
1513	**Teddy Bears & Steiff** Animals, Mandel	$9.95
1817	**Teddy Bears & Steiff** Animals, 2nd Series, Mandel	$19.95
2084	**Teddy Bears**, Annalee's & **Steiff** Animals, 3rd Series, Mandel	$19.95
1808	Wonder of **Barbie**, Manos	$9.95
1430	World of **Barbie** Dolls, Manos	$9.95
4880	World of **Raggedy Ann Collectibles**, Avery	$24.95

TOYS, MARBLES & CHRISTMAS COLLECTIBLES

3427	**Advertising Character** Collectibles, Dotz	$17.95
2333	Antique & Collectible **Marbles**, 3rd Ed., Grist	$9.95
4934	**Breyer Animal** Collector's Guide, Identification and Values, Browell	$19.95
4976	**Christmas** Ornaments, Lights & Decorations, Johnson	$24.95
4737	**Christmas** Ornaments, Lights & Decorations, Vol. II, Johnson	$24.95
4739	**Christmas** Ornaments, Lights & Decorations, Vol. III, Johnson	$24.95
2338	Collector's Encyclopedia of **Disneyana**, Longest, Stern	$24.95
4958	Collector's Guide to **Battery Toys**, Hultzman	$19.95
5038	Collector's Guide to **Diecast Toys** & Scale Models, 2nd Ed., Johnson	$19.95
4566	Collector's Guide to **Tootsietoys**, 2nd Ed, Richter	$19.95
3436	Grist's Big Book of **Marbles**	$19.95
3970	Grist's Machine-Made & Contemporary **Marbles**, 2nd Ed.	$9.95
5267	**Matchbox** Toys, 3rd Ed., 1947 to 1998, Johnson	$19.95
4871	**McDonald's** Collectibles, Henriques/DuVall	$19.95
1540	**Modern Toys** 1930–1980, Baker	$19.95
3888	**Motorcycle** Toys, Antique & Contemporary, Gentry/Downs	$18.95
5168	Schroeder's Collectible **Toys**, Antique to Modern Price Guide, 5th Ed	$17.95
1886	Stern's Guide to **Disney** Collectibles	$14.95
2139	Stern's Guide to **Disney** Collectibles, 2nd Series	$14.95
3975	Stern's Guide to **Disney** Collectibles, 3rd Series	$18.95
2028	**Toys**, Antique & Collectible, Longest	$14.95

JEWELRY, HATPINS, WATCHES & PURSES

1712	Antique & Collectible **Thimbles** & Accessories, Mathis	$19.95
1748	Antique **Purses**, Revised Second Ed., Holiner	$19.95
1278	Art Nouveau & Art Deco **Jewelry**, Baker	$9.95
4850	Collectible **Costume Jewelry**, Simonds	$24.95
3875	Collecting Antique **Stickpins**, Kerins	$16.95
3722	Collector's Ency. of **Compacts, Carryalls & Face Powder Boxes**, Mueller	$24.95
4940	**Costume Jewelry**, A Practical Handbook & Value Guide, Rezazadeh	$24.95
1716	Fifty Years of Collectible **Fashion Jewelry**, 1925-1975, Baker	$19.95
1424	**Hatpins** & Hatpin Holders, Baker	$9.95
1181	100 Years of Collectible **Jewelry**, 1850-1950, Baker	$9.95
3830	Vintage **Vanity Bags & Purses**, Gerson	$24.95

FURNITURE

1457	American **Oak** Furniture, McNerney	$9.95
3716	American **Oak** Furniture, Book II, McNerney	$12.95
1118	Antique **Oak** Furniture, Hill	$7.95
2132	Collector's Encyclopedia of **American** Furniture, Vol. I, Swedberg	$24.95
2271	Collector's Encyclopedia of **American** Furniture, Vol. II, Swedberg	$24.95
3720	Collector's Encyclopedia of **American** Furniture, Vol. III, Swedberg	$24.95
1755	Furniture of the **Depression Era**, Swedberg	$19.95
3906	**Heywood-Wakefield** Modern Furniture, Rouland	$18.95
1885	**Victorian** Furniture, Our American Heritage, McNerney	$9.95
3829	**Victorian** Furniture, Our American Heritage, Book II, McNerney	$9.95

INDIANS, GUNS, KNIVES, TOOLS, PRIMITIVES

1868	Antique **Tools**, Our American Heritage, McNerney	$9.95
1426	**Arrowheads** & Projectile Points, Hothem	$7.95
2279	**Indian** Artifacts of the Midwest, Hothem	$14.95
3885	**Indian** Artifacts of the Midwest, Book II, Hothem	$16.95
5162	Modern **Guns**, Identification & Values, 12th Ed., Quertermous	$12.95
2164	**Primitives**, Our American Heritage, McNerney	$9.95

1759	**Primitives**, Our American Heritage, Series II, McNerney	$14.95
4730	Standard **Knife** Collector's Guide, 3rd Ed., Ritchie & Stewart	$12.95 .

PAPER COLLECTIBLES & BOOKS

4633	**Big Little Books**, A Collector's Reference & Value Guide, Jacobs	$18.95
4710	Collector's Guide to **Children's Books**, 1850 to 1950, Jones	$18.95
1441	Collector's Guide to **Post Cards**, Wood	$9.95
2081	Guide to Collecting **Cookbooks**, Allen	$14.95
2080	Price Guide to **Cookbooks** & Recipe Leaflets, Dickinson	$9.95
3973	**Sheet Music** Reference & Price Guide, 2nd Ed., Pafik & Guiheen	$19.95
4654	**Victorian Trade Cards**, Historical Reference & Value Guide, Cheadle	$19.95
4733	**Whitman Juvenile Books**, Brown	$17.95

OTHER COLLECTIBLES

2269	Antique **Brass & Copper** Collectibles, Gaston	$16.95
1880	Antique **Iron**, McNerney	$9.95
3872	Antique **Tins**, Dodge	$24.95
1128	**Bottle** Pricing Guide, 3rd Ed., Cleveland	$7.95
3718	Collectible **Aluminum**, Grist	$16.95
4560	Collectible **Cats**, An Identification & Value Guide, Book II, Fyke	$19.95
4852	Collectible **Compact Disc** Price Guide 2, Cooper	$17.95
2018	Collector's Encyclopedia of **Granite Ware**, Greguire	$24.95
3430	Collector's Encyclopedia of **Granite Ware**, Book II, Greguire	$24.95
4705	Collector's Guide to Antique **Radios**, 4th Ed., Bunis	$18.95
4857	Collector's Guide to **Art Deco**, 2nd Ed., Gaston	$17.95
4933	Collector's Guide to **Bookends**, Identification & Values, Kuritzky	$19.95
3880	Collector's Guide to **Cigarette Lighters**, Flanagan	$17.95
4887	Collector's Guide to **Creek Chub Lures** & Collectibles, Smith	$24.95
3966	Collector's Guide to **Inkwells**, Identification & Values, Badders	$18.95
3881	Collector's Guide to **Novelty Radios**, Bunis/Breed	$18.95
4652	Collector's Guide to **Transistor Radios**, 2nd Ed., Bunis	$16.95
4864	Collector's Guide to **Wallace Nutting Pictures**, Ivankovich	$18.95
1629	**Doorstops**, Identification & Values, Bertoia	$9.95
3968	**Fishing Lure** Collectibles, Murphy/Edmisten	$24.95
5259	**Flea Market Trader**, 12th Ed., Huxford	$9.95
4945	**G-Men and FBI Toys**, Whitworth	$18.95
3819	**General Store** Collectibles, Wilson	$24.95
2216	**Kitchen Antiques**, 1790–1940, McNerney	$14.95
4950	The **Lone Ranger**, Collector's Reference & Value Guide, Felbinger	$18.95
2026	**Railroad** Collectibles, 4th Ed., Baker	$14.95
1632	**Salt & Pepper Shakers**, Guarnaccia	$9.95
5091	**Salt & Pepper Shakers** II, Guarnaccia	$18.95
2220	**Salt & Pepper Shakers** III, Guarnaccia	$14.95
3443	**Salt & Pepper Shakers** IV, Guarnaccia	$18.95
5007	**Silverplated Flatware**, Revised 4th Edition, Hagan	$18.95
1922	Standard **Old Bottle** Price Guide, Sellari	$14.95
3892	**Toy & Miniature Sewing Machines**, Thomas	$18.95
5057	A Treasury of **Scottie Dog** Collectibles, Davis & Baugh	$19.95
5144	Value Guide to **Advertising Memorabilia**, 2nd Ed., Summers	$19.95
3977	Value Guide to **Gas Station** Memorabilia, Summers	$24.95
4877	Vintage **Bar Ware**, Visakay	$24.95
4935	The **W.F. Cody Buffalo Bill** Collector's Guide with Values, Wojtowicz	$24.95
5281	**Wanted to Buy**, 7th Edition	$9.95

GLASSWARE & POTTERY

4929	**American Art Pottery**, 1880 – 1950, Sigafoose	$24.95
4938	Collector's Encyclopedia of **Depression Glass**, 13th Ed., Florence	$19.95
5040	Collector's Encyclopedia of **Fiesta**, 8th Ed., Huxford	$19.95
4946	Collector's Encyclopedia of **Howard Pierce Porcelain**, Dommel	$24.95
1358	Collector's Encyclopedia of **McCoy Pottery**, Huxford	$19.95
2339	Collector's Guide to **Shawnee Pottery**, Vanderbilt	$19.95
1523	Colors in **Cambridge Glass**, National Cambridge Society	$19.95
4714	**Czechoslovakian Glass** and Collectibles, Book II, Barta	$16.95
3725	**Fostoria**, Pressed, Blown & Hand Molded Shapes, Kerr	$24.95
4726	**Red Wing Art Pottery**, 1920s – 1960s, Dollen	$19.95